table of contents

table of contents

Section Three:
Safe & Healthy Food Systems

acknowledgments

Recipes for Success: a Celebration of Food Security in Canada is the result of the care and consideration of a large collective of people.

The members of the editorial committee – Herb Barbolet, Mustafa Koc, Jean-Charles LeVallee, Chris McCarville, and Todd Scarth – have provided invaluable guidance, critique and support throughout the development of this project. Don McNair was kind enough to share his knowledge and expertise as this project was first in process. The advisory committee * for The Food Project displayed patience and encouragement for a publication that grew beyond our initial expectations. The Food Project's executive committee members – Carol Ellerbeck, Paul Fieldhouse, Larry McLennan, and Terri Proulx – offered insightful suggestions on the content and form of this collection. Along with those mentioned above, Michael Heasman, Peter Reimer, and John Restakis provided valuable commentary on the introduction. Pat Sanders, our copy editor, paid great attention to detail. Jennifer Cook of Cats in the Bag Design provided her talent to ensure that this book is as enjoyable to look at, as it is to read. Ed Brajczuk of Blue Moon Graphics managed printing of this publication.

This publication was made possible by funding support from the Public Health Agency of Canada.**

Special thanks must go to all of the contributors to this collection. It is their stories, work and dedication to the issue of food security that provides inspiration for all of us.

*The Food Project Advisory Committee members are:

- Jody Andrews, EarthShare Cooperative Farm
- Derek Pachal, United Way of Winnipeg
- Terri Proulx, SEED Winnipeg
- Sheryl Bates Dancho, Winnipeg Regional Health Authority
- Carol Ellerbeck, Winnipeg Harvest
- Sharon Taylor, Wolseley Family Place
- Ted McLachlan, Department of Landscape Architecture, University of Manitoba
- Viola Prowse, Manitoba Council on Child Nutrition
- Jan Smith, River East Transcona School Division
- Pat Lachance, Population Health, Public Health Agency of Canada
- Paul Fieldhouse, Manitoba Health and Healthy Living
- Genny Funk-Unrau, St. Mathews Maryland Healthy Living Committee
- Larry McLennan, Manitoba Restaurant Association
- Laura Donatelli, Diabetes Prevention, Public Health Agency of Canada
- Nigel Basely, West Broadway Development Corporation

**The views expressed in this publication are the author's and do not necessarily reflect the opinions of the Public Health Agency of Canada or of the federal government.

foreword

Recipes for Success creates an opportunity for us to review and celebrate the unfolding story of the food security movement in Canada. And what a good story it is! Food security work in Canada has come a long way. There are many chapters in this story.

I was a part of some of the early chapters when food banks and emergency food assistance as we know it now were just beginning and when the concept of food security was a way to broaden our analysis and action. I am excited to see in these recipes for success all the energy, innovation and vision that has grown from such modest beginnings.
So many more and diverse actors are involved. Note that these recipes for success are not the first nor last chapters in the story - they have grown from chapters written in the 1980s and carry within them the seeds for the closing chapter when indeed every person will have ready access to enough quality food for an active, healthy life through a sustainable food system that maximizes community self-reliance and social justice.

But here in the midst of this story, it is good to take a moment to celebrate the commitment, vision, perseverance, compassion and understanding contained in these accounts. They say much about love of the earth, love of neighbour, and a passion for health, justice and a caring economy.

Yet, this work is very tangible and accomplished in real time in communities of all kinds from sea to sea. These accounts are fabulous antidotes to the cynicism, fatalism and negativity that saturate our environments. Connecting with the local food security network is an excellent way to dispel disheartenment with the current state of our world. This is a true grassroots, bottom-up account of civil society helping to make our society civil. Without this web of constructive caring, the lives of many Canadians would be significantly harsher.

It is also good to honour the people behind these accounts. They are wonderful, diverse representatives of the much larger group of people who make up this movement. We have much to give thanks for in their leadership and support of this work. And we have much to urge our governments and foundations to support. They say the best compliment is imitation, so it is fabulous to have such recipes to follow and upon which to elaborate.

As good as it is to celebrate our recipes for success, it is critical to remember and be challenged by the insecurity, poverty, environmental degradation, disorder and monopolistic distortions in our current food system. Real people in real communities have compromised health, well-being and futures because of individual and collective food insecurity. There is much yet to do for our collective table where everyone has a place and with every place respected. These recipes for success are good fertilizer for our ongoing work. Thanks to all who submitted accounts of their work and to those who compiled and made this recipe book live.

Reverend Dr. Cathy C. Campbell
Rector, St.Matthew's Anglican Church, Winnipeg author of Stations of the Banquet: Faith Foundations for Food Justice

introduction

It is tempting to begin this introduction with some reference to food banks. After all, the origin of the food security movement as a modern concern in Canada is marked by their emergence in the 1980's. For many working in this field, this has been seen as a watershed moment marking significant socio-economic change in our country. And in fact the persistence and expansion of food banks into the present day has made this change seem irreversible.

Food - which is intimately connected to all aspects of our personal and social well-being - is fundamentally influenced by the economic and social policies that govern our society. Shifts in these policies occurring over these last decades have had a profound impact on the reality of food at both a personal and social level. The implementation of market policies without accountability to those most intimately affected has had profound effects on the weakening of social conditions in communities across Canada and around the globe.

Like the Industrial Revolution, globalization is a cultural transformation as much as it is a change in the way of doing business. Rapid technological development and the re-emergence of the ideology of laissez-faire economics fostered the conditions for a restructuring of the fabric of Canadian society. This doctrine of market liberalism took hold in the 1980's and has expanded through the 1990's and into the 21st century.

Food banks and the growth in food security initiatives were a community-based response to a growing food crisis in our country that was one result of such policies. For just as they influence large-scale systems, economic systems have a very human impact at a local level.

Food issues are rarely divorced form wider changes in society. In the space of two generations we have become a society that relies almost exclusively on an industrialized, globalized food system to meet our most basic of human needs. We worry that our children may not know where our food comes from; indeed how many of us really know the where and how of the food production and processing system that is behind Sunday dinner? Achieving this knowledge is no easy task. Add to the increasing concentration and consolidation in the agri-food industry the scarcity of time many of us experience and it seems more difficult to negotiate our way through grocery store aisles and food labels to find food that we can feel good about putting on the table. And as the proliferation of food banks reminds us, too many in our communities have to make a shrinking food budget stretch further and further.

For many working in this field, food security is about ensuring access to nutritious and culturally appropriate food in a manner that promotes human dignity. But we also know food security is about much more than this. It's about promoting social justice, sustainable food production, healthy food habits and community-based, democratically-controlled solutions to the issues of hunger, malnutrition and a distorted food system. And this is where Recipes for Success comes in. It is an attempt to profile and celebrate the array of activity in Canada occurring under the banner of food security.

How this book came about has a story behind it as well. Some time ago members of the local organizing committee for the National Food Security Assembly 2004 were discussing ways to celebrate work in the area of food security taking place throughout the country.

What better way to do this, we thought, *than to share the stories of assembly participants in a publication of some kind?* Following the Assembly this idea matured, and we were fortunate to have the opportunity to incorporate it into our work with The Food Project in Winnipeg.

This collection of stories has been organized into sections that parallel the priorities of Food Secure Canada (FSC), a new national food security organization. Section One contains stories that focus on Social Justice and Hunger Alleviation. Contributions to this section are from community based organizations, food banks and faith groups covering topics as varied as innovative fund raising and public awareness initiatives to community economic development. Section Two gathers examples of work towards Sustainable Food Systems. In here you will find stories ranging from small-scale organic farms to provincial networks and co-ops. Section Three has Safe and Healthy Food Systems as the organizing theme. Submissions to this section include school salad bars, a bid from a university student society to run food services and participatory action research.

Our hope is that in the face of alarming statistics regarding increasing obesity, chronic disease, and food bank use-not to mention the sometimes dire situation facing farming and fishing communities in our country-this collection of stories will serve to highlight the responses to these issues by individuals, organizations, enterprises and communities. As these stories demonstrate, to be effective food security work needs to operate at multiple levels - individual, community, society - and in multiple arenas - political, cultural and economic. The experiences and knowledge contained within should serve to inspire us to realize that meaningful action is possible and that concrete alternatives to our current state of affairs are numerous and diverse.

It is important to note that this collection is not intended to be comprehensive nor is it representative of all the work going on across the country. But it is a place to begin to take stock of the breadth and depth of food security activity in Canada and to recognize the role we all play in responding to social needs.

We hope that these stories will motivate and inspire you as much as they have us.

Anna Maria Kirbyson
Coordinator
The Food
Project

section one: Social Justice and Hunger Alleviation

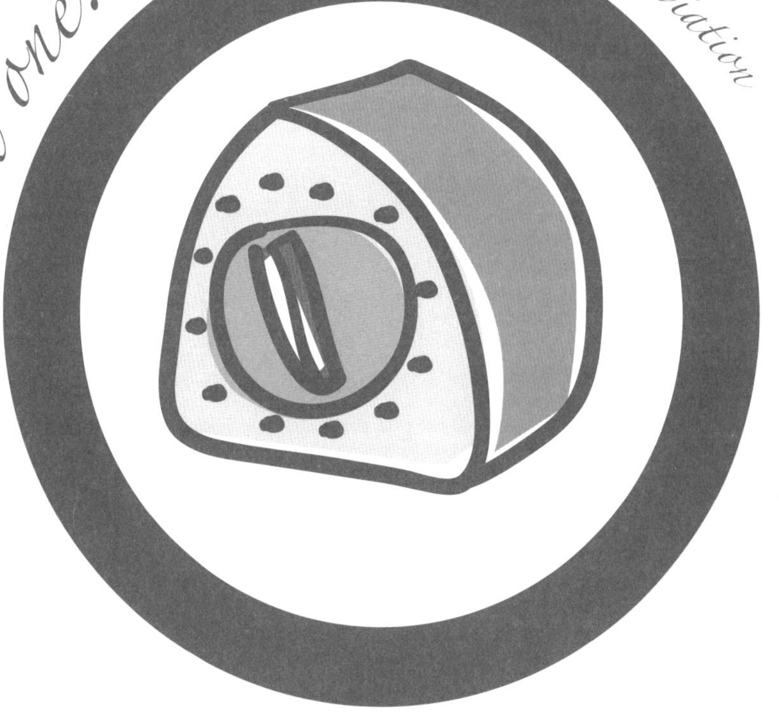

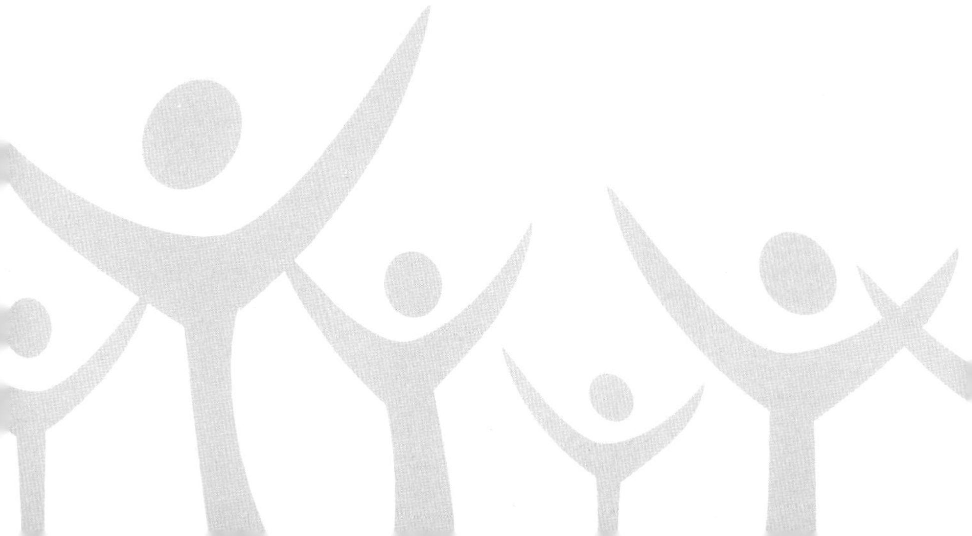

The West Broadway Good Food Club

*Living in Harmony
with the Earth and Each Other*
by Meagan Peasgood

Established as a response to the needs of inner-city residents, the Good Food Club is still going strong three years into the life of the program. This home-grown initiative is ripe with grassroots action and opportunities for education, empowerment and inclusion.

It all stemmed from the efforts of an inter-agency coalition of health and social workers who had been meeting to develop strategies for better food access in West Broadway. The first batch of funding was given by the Winnipeg Foundation and Neighbourhoods Alive! for a Good Food Box program targeting neighbourhood people who frequented food banks, souplines and drop-ins.

As people were invited to participate, it was clear there was little to no enthusiasm in the community for a Good Food Box. The idea that an individual could commit 15 or 20 dollars from an already stretched budget was unrealistic.

A variety of community consultation methods ensued. Many dreams and ideas were put forward for programming. That first gathering of low-income residents and the sharing of their experiences uniquely shaped what the Good Food Club has become today. It was at these early meetings that the core values of the Good Food Club were established:

1) Affordable–Food must be low in price, and offered at a location to which people could walk.

2) Enjoyable–Whatever the event, it had to be intentionally community building.

3) Nutritious–Food must be nutritious to improve health and diabetes conditions.

The current membership of the Good Food Club is very diverse, reflecting the nature of the West Broadway community itself. Members abundantly reflect a variety of ethnic origins, age / income groups, spiritual perspectives, sexual orientations, and physical / mental abilities. This diversity has at times been a struggle, but has since proved to be enlightening for all members. The cohesive nature of the GFC and its capacity for relationship building is deeply rooted within the differences of member to member. Opportunities continue to arise for members to develop a deeper cross-cultural understanding of one another.

As a community development model, the Good Food Club seeks to:

• Facilitate education about nutrition and food access.

• Demonstrate that care and cultivation of the earth is synonymous with care and cultivation of one another and one's self.

• Engage participants in the Food Security discussion by helping them to see food as their human right, and by doing so, to encourage them to become food activists. It dispels the myth that while people generate little or no income, they are powerless to have an impact on current food systems.

• Provide practical applications to the phrase " Think Globally, Act Locally."

• Model interconnectedness: Healthy economics, healthy relationships, and healthy food = healthy people and healthy communities.

The Good Food Club program stretches into a variety of areas including Cooking Classes, Community Kitchens, Workshops, and Catering. There are five main areas of action:

1) In the summer months, the GFC becomes an active part of a family farm with the generous help and mentoring of our good friends at the Wiens Family Shared Farm. Anyone with a membership to the Good Food Club can come out to spend a day digging in the soil, interacting with farm folk, and learning by immersion valuable skills that have an impact on their understanding of the value of whole, green foods. Once some of the crop becomes ready to harvest each Saturday the infamous VEGGIE VAN (a 1987 Dodge painted with loud, funky cartoon veggies and fruits)rolls up to the local community centre with fresh vegetables to sell at a very low cost to people in the neighbourhood. In this mini farmer's market environment, food is sold cheaply to all people in the community, but GFC members get first access.

When we look back over a season at the farm, there are a few instant impressions: searing heat; romaine lettuce so big and luxurious they could be used as bridal bouquets; sharing sandwiches in the field that are filled only with things we grew ourselves; mud up to the knees; a nine year old boy holding up a tomato and asking "what is this thing?"; heated debate over where to deposit the multitude of cigarette butts generated while working in the rows; beetles consuming all but one or two cabbage plants; a mother with six children in tow who is crying as she fills her veggie bags.

2) In the fall and winter members of the Good Food Club host "community cafes." These feast-like events are organized, cooked, served, decorated, and even entertained by our very own community folks. It is not an uncommon sight to see one of the cooks dart for the stage and take up a guitar to serenade the café guests. Members of the Good Food Club spend time planning together on various committees to create a special community gathering that provides a wholesome and nutritious meal in an appealing atmosphere. Linens, dishes and candles all help to create a healthy restaurant feeling, without being inaccessible to low-income budgets.

A café is a chance for many individuals to be served at table, as opposed to standing in a soup line. Cafes create a time and place to celebrate the gifts each individual can contribute to their community. Here are some more tangential impressions from the mind's eye: 35 people jostling around each other in a scorching kitchen with dance-like movements, "this is SO much better than the soup kitchen"; basmati rice exploding all over a double range; the suggestion that potlucks conclude with a discussion group (our first one was about welfare rights, led by a resident living on assistance); a mental health survivor who struggles with confidence reading aloud a poem she wrote about her psychiatrist; a highly coveted pair of salad tongs and sequined cowboy hat at the annual holiday Gift-O-Rama (where you swap surprise presents; lineups of hungry people urging us to open the café early; spontaneous sing-a-longs (valdaree, valdarah…); a table of seven to ten year old boys inhaling gobs of beans and spinach without a shred of complaint; local musicians (professionals and amateurs) sharing songwriting techniques; an evening where, by pure coincidence, there appeared 12 identical casseroles, a lonely Jello pudding sitting amongst the potluck offerings; stretching portions to the limi, then feeling sick at having to turn people away when the food is sold out; tired feet and backs from hunching over the dish-pit; from the same mouth "this looks disgusting" to "that was amazing, can I have the recipe"; it goes on and on.

3) Once a week residents gather to share a meal together as part of our POTLUCK CLUB. Each person brings food to share with everyone, a casserole, salad, bread, fruit or vegetables. The encouragement is for each individual to bring what they can. Help is available for people who need assistance with getting recipes, ingredients or a place to cook.

The emphasis is on the act of contributing, regardless of the amount. The potlucks are also a great opportunity for people to cook together, share ideas for recipes and gain awareness of other food lifestyles.

4) Once a month members can place orders in a bulk-purchasing program called the GOOD FOOD BOX.

The Good Food Box is a simple and affordable way to get fresh fruits and vegetables. Each month the members receive a recyclable box (home delivered) containing a variety of food they ordered a few weeks before. As much as possible, Manitoba-grown produce is selected. With each custom order, a member can pay the discount price of bulk food buying, without having to buy a large amount of food. Included in each box are simple recipes and GFC newsletters.

5) When an individual becomes a member of the Good Food Club, they become eligible to earn SWEAT EQUITY POINTS by volunteering their time at a GFC event. Farm work, potlucks, cafés and Good Food Box packing are some of the ways members can accumulate points. Sweat Equity points are the Good Food Clubs' barter currency, and can be used as dollars towards the purchase of a Good Food Box.

The Good Food Club's work comes closer to articulating a spirituality of food than community development. It is seen in the difference we make every time residents gather to share a meal with one another - knowing many of those in attendance are considered shut-ins. It is seen in a GFC farmers' eye when a crop they helped to nurture is brought in from the field - when everything about the city tells them they have nothing to offer society. Most importantly, however, it is seen amongst the crowds that show up for the Veggie van - to stock their fridges and cupboards with the harvest.

The Cost of Eating in BC

by Shefali Raja

Dietitians and their community partners in British Columbia are increasingly concerned about the ability of those on low incomes, especially families on income assistance, to access safe and healthy food in a dignified manner. An unhealthy diet, along with other lifestyle risk factors, contributes significantly to the main killers in BC – diabetes, heart disease, cancer and respiratory disease. In addition, living on a low income puts British Columbians at an even greater risk of dying from these diseases. The gap between the cost of living and social assistance amounts continues to grow. It is important to communicate this to policy makers.

"The Cost of Eating in BC" is a report that highlights the cost per month for a family to eat a healthy diet. It is used to demonstrate percentages of disposable income spent on of food among families of various sizes and incomes. It clearly shows the limited monies left over and, in some scenarios, no monies left over to cover other basic living expenses for those with low incomes or on assistance. The report includes research on the link between food-insecure individuals and the social determinants of health.

The report also addresses how individuals can empower themselves and make changes at the community level. Finally, the report makes recommendations to address food security at a policy level.

To determine the cost of healthy eating, registered dietitians working in public health across the province price a nutritious food basket using Health Canada's standardized food costing tool, the National Nutritious Food Basket 1998. Dietitians cost 66 food items from stores across BC. The Nutritious Food Basket consists of low-cost basic foods from all the four food groups and reflects the typical purchasing patterns of Canadian families. It does not include expensive, convenience-type foods or other necessities like hygiene products. The monthly cost to feed the reference family of four (two parents, two children) a basic diet was $632 in 2004. A low income family would need to spend up to 42% of their disposable income on a nutritious diet, compared to the average Canadian with one earner spending 16%. That's unreasonable and not achievable. To survive, families would be forced to seek out poor housing in unsafe neighbourhoods, line up at food banks and soup kitchens, leave their children in unsafe child care situations due to the high cost of child care and go without the basic necessities of life, including healthy food.

Food security is an essential precursor to an active, healthy lifestyle. Since the causes and impacts of food insecurity are multi-factorial, strategies and policies that enable food security, and ultimately healthy eating, span the mandates of many ministries, sectors and jurisdictions. Collaboration among key players, including BC ministries (Human Resources, Education, Health Services, Community, Aboriginal and Women's Services, Children and Family Development) and BC Health Authorities, concerned organization and citizens, is needed to determine effective, long-term solutions to poverty and food insecurity.

The report makes recommendations on how to work towards achieving food security for BC families:

- Better employment and wage rates are key to reducing poverty.

- Government taxes and transfers can have a significant effect on reducing low income.

- An effective child-benefit system is necessary, one that provides enough income support to keep working parents out of poverty, one that is not clawed back by the provincial government for those on income assistance.

- Adequate provincial income assistance rates should be based on a reasonable cost of living.

- More affordable housing is necessary to end homelessness and enable parents to raise their children in healthy community environments.

- Increased support is necessary for programs such as Community LINK (Learning Includes Nutrition and Knowledge), now under the mandate of the Ministry of Education, which provides services and supports in schools for vulnerable children and youth, including school meal programs and inner-city programs.

The report has been an annual project written by Dietitians of Canada BC Region and Community Nutritionists' Council of BC. It is endorsed by several agencies including the Social Planning and Research Council of BC, Health Officers' Council of BC, BC Healthy Living Alliance, Public Health Association of BC, BC Association of Social Workers, etc. It is required reading in some of the courses offered at UBC and is also used as a reference by others and draws national attention. We have also had the opportunity to meet with several of the BC ministers to discuss the recommendations and will continue to advocate for the most vulnerable in our population. A copy of the report can be downloaded from Dietitians of Canada's Resource Centre at: www.dietitians.ca.

Le Magasins-Partage
by Nathalie Dupuis

History

It was in December of 1986, at Patro le Prévost in Montréal's Villeray area, that the precursor of the Christmas Helping-Hand Store was born. At the time, it served 35 families. This local initiative sparked the interest of other groups seeking an alternative to the customary Christmas hampers. They were dissatisfied and felt uncomfortable handing out food in conditions in which the donor-recipient relationship fostered prejudice, dependence, inaction and indifference. And so it was that in 1993, in the context of the Metropolitan Montréal IssueTable on Hunger, the committee for Magasins-Partage was struck.

In 1995, an initial attempt to make group purchases was carried out. The first co-ordinator was hired in 1996 to head the primary Christmas drive. In 1998 the Regroupement des Magasins-Partage de l'Île de Montréal became a legally constituted, not-for-profit organization and was given charitable organization status.

Helping Hands Stores

The warm and friendly atmosphere of the Helping Hands Stores is reminiscent of the corner grocery stores of yesteryear.

They are a significant alternative to emergency food aid since they:

• Give destitute people the power to choose their own food. Food items are set out so that the Helping Hands Store physically resembles a grocery store. Participants (destitute people) can shop like everyone else and put the food they want to eat into their carts. It is important that the tastes and culture of participants are respected.

• Enable participants to contribute up to ten percent of the value of their food baskets and thus become stakeholders in a group project. By allowing participants to make a small contribution for their purchases, we make it possible for them to perform a civic act with dignity by acquiring food in exchange for a contribution. Moreover, these funds are immediately reinvested into the Helping Hands Store, thus enabling participants to help others.

• Are local food security projects organized primarily through the joint action of organizations and their partners within the same territory. All the players within a single territory are invited to become involved in running a Helping Hands Store, be they from the community-based, public, parapublic or business world. This makes it possible to make community as a whole more aware of the poverty experienced by its fellow citizens.

• Invite participants to volunteer, thus giving them the opportunity to break through their social isolation and experience solidarity in a positive way. Involving participants as volunteers gives them the chance to rub elbows with workers from all walks of life and perform the same tasks they do. This experience heightens participants' self-esteem.

• Are gateways to a self-help network since organizers follow up on registered individuals by directing them to the resources most likely to help them gain empowerment.

Because the Helping Hands stores are organized through the joint action of groups, their participants come into direct contact with workers from different walks of life and can thus begin immediately to build up bonds of trust. Participants are referred to the resources that can help them (self-help groups, ACEF, collective kitchens, purchasing groups, housing committees, etc.).

Being careful not to create a new emergency food aid service that gives rise to dependence or even second-rate grocery stores, the Helping Hands stores take in participants at two strategic times in the year: the back-to-school period and the Christmas season.

The Christmas Helping Hands Store provides participants with special food for the holiday season along with a wide array of other food items. Free toys, books and various gifts are also available.

The Christmas Helping Hands Stores are open from December 15 to 22, as it is thought that if participants get their food items before December 15, they will no longer have enough left to celebrate Christmas. After December 22, participants will not have time to organize the season's celebrations with dignity.

The Back-to-School Helping Hands Store offers families a week's worth of food, focussing on breakfast and lunch-box fare.

Furthermore, the children of these families are invited to choose the school bag, school supplies and insulated lunch box they like and need.

To ensure that the children already have their school supplies by the time school starts, the Helping Hands Stores are open the week before the beginning of the school year.

Le Regroupement

The Regroupement des Magasins-Partage de l'Île de Montréal is now a major player in Montréal's food security. It ensures that the original concept of Helping Hands Stores is honoured and enhanced. It is also a place for all its members to meet, exchange ideas, organize and speak out.

Regroupement Activities

Le Regroupement's main activity is to conduct fundraising drives for its members. The money raised is used for group purchases of food and school supplies, which are then redistributed through the network of Helping Hands Stores to complement local fundraisers.

Other activities are also part of the Regroupement des Magasins-Partage:
• Conducting media campaigns;
• Promoting the concept;
• Guiding new members;
• Following up on members;
• Fundraising;
• Developing partnerships; and
• Joint action.

A Democratic Place

Meeting once a month, Helping Hands Store members play an important role in the decisions made and the directions taken by the Regroupement.

The Regroupement, A Force to Be Reckoned With

Growing from the 35 families Villeray took in back in 1986, the Regroupement and its members now support 7000 households spread across the various areas of Montréal. This amounts to 17,500 people who, each year, profit from grocery purchases at the Christmas and back-to-school seasons.

thINK FOOD/
Phones-for-Food Project
by Chokey Tsering

Founded in 1985, the Canadian Association of Food Banks (CAFB) is the national umbrella organization representing voluntary food charities. CAFB is the voice of food banks in Canada, with approximately 240 members and their respective agencies serving about 90% of people accessing emergency food programs nation-wide. CAFB relies on a nationwide network of volunteers, corporations and donations. The CAFB:

- acts as advocates for food bank users and publishes HungerCount, an annual survey of food bank use in Canada
- distributes large food donations to member banks through the National Food Sharing System with voluntary transportation
- promotes the dignity of food bank users and the ethical stewardship of donated food
- surveys Canadians' perceptions of the problem of hunger
- works with food banks, corporations and government to solve Canada's growing hunger problem

Since 1997, the CAFB has been closely monitoring trends in food bank use through its annual HungerCount study, a leading barometer of hunger, poverty and food insecurity in Canada.

The only national survey of its kind in Canada, the study provides information that is used throughout the year by those in community-based organizations, government, research, media and the corporate sector.

Food banks have experienced first-hand how responses to food insecurity over the years have largely been community-based and ad hoc in nature. Since the opening of the first food bank in 1981, they have become institutionalized in Canadian society. The latest HungerCount findings show that food bank use has reached a record high. These alarming trends point to the need to broaden and strengthen coordinated action within the food security network.

In recognition of this need, CAFB helped sponsor and participated in the 2004 Food Security Assembly in Winnipeg, Manitoba. It was enormously inspired by the convergence of those from all sectors of the food security field with the desire to facilitate partnerships and build on existing work.

thINK FOOD / Phones-for-Food

The thINK FOOD / Phones-for-Food project is an ongoing environmental fundraising and educational program serving the interests and mandate of the CAFB, respective provincial food bank associations and their community food bank members. The first national program of its kind in Canada, the project has a mission to alleviate hunger and divert waste from landfill sites. The project raises funds for community food banks through the process of recycling used printer cartridges and cell phones.

Having originally begun in early 2001 as a cartridge-recycling fundraiser for Toronto's Daily Bread Food Bank, the project was made available across the province with the sponsorship support of Petro-Canada and the Ontario Association of Food Banks. In response to its burgeoning popularity among food banks and the general public, in April 2002 the CAFB launched the project nationally, with the support of sponsors and partners. The launch made the project available to all food banks and communities across the country. In March 2003, Purolator became a national sponsor and the collection of cell phones was initiated with the roll-out of the Phones-for-Food project. Rogers Wireless set up the project in their stores and announced their national sponsorship of thINK FOOD / Phones-for-Food in October 2004.

Today this award-winning project has generated more than 300,000 pounds of food with the collection of more than 200,000 printer cartridges and almost 50,000 cell phones. The project was the recipient of the Canadian Centre for Philanthropy's 2003 Imagine "New Spirit of Community" award and the Recycling Council of Ontario's 2002/2003 Waste Minimization Award. More recently, the project was named a finalist for the 2005 Canadian Environment Awards – a partnership between the Government of Canada and Canadian Geographic Enterprises. Thousands of businesses, schools and government offices are established as collection sites in support of hundreds of local food banks across Canada.

Beneficiaries: Food Banks
The unrestricted funds that are generated can be spent by local community food banks on their greatest needs. On average, one cartridge or cell phone equals a carton of milk, a jar of peanut butter or even a whole meal.

Other benefits to food banks include:
• Little labour and no expenses required from the non-profits
• Expansion of donor database through the development of new contacts
• Opportunity to expand relationship with current donors
• Exposure of hunger and environmental issues to new audience

The Environment
With landfills quickly reaching maximum capacity and community groups seeking alternative means of funding, the project is a creative

response to these two growing problems. Harmful waste is diverted from the garbage every time someone recycles their used inkjet cartridge or cell phone. Keeping the cartridges and cell phones out of the landfill is important because:

• The plastic casings from printer cartridges take thousands of years to decompose

• The ink residue from the cartridges leaks into the water tables

• 2.5 to 4 ounces of oil is used for every new cartridge casing that is made

• Nickel cadmium batteries used in cell phones are hazardous

• Reusing cell phones means that expensive mineral and mining processes with harsh environmental effects can be lessened or avoided.

Broad Support, Grassroots Growth
There are over 4500 collection sites registered with the project in more than 400 Canadian communities. These sites truly represent every sector, including churches, community organizations, schools and universities, retail and small business, service clubs, community centres, grocery stores, banks, large corporate offices, manufacturing plants and all levels of government. The majority of registered sites have signed up unsolicited and have never recycled their cell phones or printer cartridges before participating in this project.

Forging Local Partnerships
Genuine and diverse partnerships are at the core of this project's development. The project has attracted the attention and support of a variety of local partners who have gone the extra mile to make it successful in their community:

• The City of Toronto set up public collection sites at community centres and featured the project in their Environment Days.

• The Kinsmen Club in Halifax took a direct interest in promoting the project to new sites.

13

- Elementary schools in Beamsville hosted a friendly collection competition.

- The Chamber of Commerce in Alberta made a concerted effort to encourage Chambers of Commerce across the province to participate.

- The Girl Guides joining forces with the City of Regina to promote the project door-to-door in their community.

Grassroots Public Education

Despite having a very little advertising budget, the project has garnered approximately five million dollars in PR value from media and other publicity opportunities. In addition to community media events, this has been primarily thanks to project supporters who spread the word by posting information on their Web Sites, in their newsletters, in their workplaces and schools, or simply by telling a friend.

By invitation, the project has also been showcased at numerous conferences and forums including: the Ministry of the Environment's Pollution Prevention Round Table; the Association of Municipal Recyclers Coordinators Conference; the Saskatchewan Waste Reduction Council Conference; the Environmental and Social Action Conference: York University; and the Creating Sustainable Communities Conference for Youth.

Conclusion

A successful food security initiative thINK FOOD/Phones-for-Food has encouraged recycling behaviour in communities across Canada and has generated significant dollars for much-needed emergency food programs. It is an initiative that is integrative and encompasses multiple goals characteristic of food security initiatives:

- It forges inter-sectoral partnerships (between local communities, including food banks, and business) and thus promotes coalition building within a broader, common goal;

- It negates the ad hoc nature of responses to food security issues, such as hunger, by being purposeful and deliberate in its activities and intent.

The project is an unprecedented example of an effective public education vehicle, driven by public support, for fostering awareness of hunger and environmental issues through unique community partnerships. It is balanced by having both a national infrastructure (national sponsorship, centralized management), and community-specific implementation and partnerships (food banks can tailor the program in accordance with their local conditions and relationships).

As a non-profit organization that regularly struggles to mobilize efforts to fight hunger, this latter feature of the project has been a valuable educational experience for the CAFB. Social justice groups have long been familiar with the challenges of fostering committed and effective public support for attacking the underlying social and economic conditions that generate hunger, poverty and food insecurity. Notwithstanding these barriers, there also remain obstacles within the food security field itself to creating cohesive alliances. Considering the diverse landscape within the field, forming enduring intra-sectoral partnerships has been slow to achieve since it entails, to some extent, cutting across inherent ideological and structural disparities among existing groups.

However, in light of the unrelenting social, economic and health problems linked to food insecurity, forging multi-sectoral and multi-tiered initiatives has never been more urgent. The thINK FOOD/Phones-for-Food is proof that such collective efforts are not only possible, but that they can be extremely successful. It demonstrates that a cooperative undertaking – one that capitalizes on existing differences – can deliver more far-reaching rewards than any singular effort.

Food Security within a Manitoba Housing Community

*Woodydell Family
Resource Centre – A Community
Outreach Program of the Family Centre*

by Maureen Barchyn

*"It's helping with my cooking and being
better at making meals. We have a cookbook
and they provide a basic shelf hamper so that
way you can start from what you have.
It's healthier and cheaper and I'm getting
better at making meals."*

The Family Centre, in partnership
with Manitoba Housing Authority, has
established the Woodydell Family Resource
Centre in a regional housing complex in
St. Vital. Manitoba Housing provides the
space and The Family Centre provides the
staffing to facilitate programs for parents
and children. The partnership began in
2002, at the request of the tenants, so that
they could have programming and support
that was readily accessible to families in
their own complex.

A Tenants' Advisory Committee
meets regularly to assess community
needs, resolve problems and plan programs
that meet the needs of the community.
Through a variety of programs being
offered, the hope is to enhance parenting
skills, promote positive relationships
between parents and children, improve
basic life skills and enable neighbours to
meet one another and form a stronger,
healthier community.

*"It's a great place to come and connect
with people. It helps me to be aware of all
the resources in my community for me
as a single mother."*

Community Kitchen

The majority of the families
living in the Woodydell
community live in poverty.
Making ends meet between
paycheques is an ongoing
challenge. In addition, many
parents don't have the basic skills
to plan and prepare low-cost
nutritious meals. The goal at
Woodydell is to build community
capacity. One of the first needs identified
by the Tenants Advisory Committee
was get a community kitchen up and
running. The program started out with one
community kitchen each week and then a
second program was added, later in the day,
to accommodate families who are working
or going to school. Each family arrives
with an empty pot or casserole dish and
two dollars as a contribution to food costs.

*"I found out about the Woodydell
Resource Centre by word of mouth. At
first, I came for the Community Kitchen.
For two dollars you can prepare a nutritious
meal. We all get together and you leave with
enough portions to feed your whole family. It's
a friendly environment where you get to meet
neighbours - a very good place."*

The Resource Centre relies on regular
deliveries from Winnipeg Harvest, a
local food bank, to offset food costs.
Everyone works together the day of the
community kitchen to make the menu
items in large quantities. Usually this
includes a low-cost main dish, vegetable
or bread product and often a dessert.
Parents take home enough dinner to feed
their families that evening plus the new
skill of making a nutritious dinner from
scratch. Some of the favourites have
included: beef stir fry, corn bread, chili,
spaghetti with meat sauce, herb baked
chicken, minestrone soup, apple crisp
and bannock.

Basic Shelf Hampers

"There are single fathers out here that need this program. I think every complex in Manitoba Housing should have these centres. Single fathers and mothers need this."

Once the community kitchens were operational, another obstacle to food security became obvious. Staples such as sugar, flour, baking powder, oatmeal, rice, canned goods and spices form the basis for many meals. However, families often did not have the basic cooking supplies in their own kitchens to prepare meals from scratch. In addition, mixing bowls and measuring cups and spoons were often non-existent. Purchasing a supply of staples is a huge expense for a low-income family but having this basic shelf of staples on hand is often what makes the difference between a full stomach and going without when money runs short at the end of the month. The Tenants' Advisory Committee, under the direction of The Family Centre staff, decided to provide families who attended community kitchen on a regular basis with a basic shelf hamper to take home. It included a supply of the foods listed above as well as some simple utensils and a cookbook. Funds were obtained to purchase the hampers through donations.

Community Cupboard

"It's great to be able to buy a roll of toilet paper for 25 cents."

It's the day before payday and you're out of dish soap, diapers or toilet paper. What do you do? The Community Cupboard that operates out of the Woodydell Family Resource Centre is similar to a general store and sells small quantities of basic household items at cost. Laundry soap, flour, tins of soup, peanut butter and pasta can be purchased on-site. It's a way to "tide families over" until they are able to go grocery shopping. The store has been organized and staffed by community volunteers. A start-up grant was obtained at the outset to purchase a basic inventory and the Community Cupboard is now self-sustaining.

Welcome to New Families

"They also bring cookies to new neighbours. They did that for me and that was nice. That's how I got to know people here."

When a new family moves into the community, Manitoba Housing staff notifies the staff at Woodydell Family Resource Centre. Staff and volunteers work together to make a welcoming gift of freshly baked cookies and then a member of the community delivers it to the home of the new tenant. When they drop the cookies off, they also provide information about the centre and extend an invitation to drop by.

Second Site at St. Anne's Family Resource Centre

In November 2004, The Family Centre entered into a second partnership with Manitoba Housing to open another site in a St. Vital housing complex. The first community kitchen at this site began in January 2005 and the tenant response has been very positive.

"You can have coffee, chat and meet your neighbours. The staff are willing to talk to you and guide you; they're very supportive."

In summary, the Woodydell and St. Anne's Family Resource Centers address empowerment and community capacity building at the grassroots level. Having the knowledge, ability and resources to provide nutritious food for your family is a basic right of every individual in society to ensure health and well-being. Initiatives like the food security programs being offered at Woodydell and St. Anne's provide families with the opportunity to begin to take control of their lives and their community.

"Happy parents mean happy kids. We do have our ups and downs. When you're a single parent, reaching out to others makes your community a little bigger. These places are important and they're really needed."

LITE and Food Security in Winnipeg's Inner City

Hampers would still be delivered to those in need. However the staff at Neechi Foods would stay employed (not adding to the list of hamper recipients). This way one inner-city business would benefit from the generosity of Winnipeggers.

This was just the beginning of many food-oriented projects that LITE supports. Neechi Foods continues to operate in the heart of the North End of Winnipeg – offering healthy alternatives, locally produced jams, cheese, meats, bannock, salads and more. LITE continues to purchase over $30,000 of groceries each year from Neechi Foods for the hamper program during the holidays.

by Karen Schlichting

Good food is becoming hard to find and good food in the inner city of Winnipeg harder still. Healthy, locally grown food is an even more rare bird. Local Investment Toward Employment (LITE) has been investing in community economic development (CED) projects that engage the neighbourhoods' employment needs since 1994. LITE started its fundraising initiative around food as a response to issues arising from the free Christmas food hampers being distributed to inner-city residents during the holiday season. As more hampers were being distributed, a locally owned Aboriginal worker co-op in the heart of the 'hamper zone' was realizing that the holiday season was putting them out of business. Neechi Foods, committed to hiring local residents, providing affordable healthy food and locally produced items when available, could not compete with all the free food that flooded its neighbourhood.

As a result, a group of concerned citizens started the LITE Campaign. They asked Winnipegers to donate to LITE during the holiday season. The donations were used to purchase food from Neechi Foods and deliver it to the Winnipeg Cheer Board, the organization that provides the hampers.

Throughout the year, LITE supports several other inventive community groups – seeking healthier, more meaningful options to food consumption and production in the inner city. Several community groups have blended their need for income generation and food security. The result was food, fabulous food!

St. Matthews Maryland Community Garden Preserves has taken over some vacant lots and started growing gardens. Out of these gardens, people are learning how to prepare the food they are growing. They produce jams, cater meals and sell a range of products they put together themselves. They are learning how to access, grow and cook healthy food and they are employed and employable in the process!

In the West Broadway Neighbourhood, the brightly painted 'veggie van' is another sign of life springing out of great food. The Good Food Club is a community project that brings inner-city residents to the Weins Shared Family Farm just on the outskirts of Winnipeg. Inner-city residents join in the planting and harvesting of produce and bring a van full of affordable organic veggies to the street corners in the neighbourhood.

Local residents learn how to grow, sell, prepare food, organize potlucks and community cafés – where they share their recipes and new ways of 'doing' food.

Club members who volunteer to head out to the farm for the day earn sweat equity points, which can then be used to purchase food at a highly discounted price.

To distribute the produce, which includes everything from carrots to onions, peppers and tomatoes, the 'veggie van' is loaded up on Saturdays and driven to the local community centre. Like a mini farmer's market, the van opens at noon and closes when the veggies are all gone – which usually takes about 20 minutes. Club members pay $2, low-income neighbours and students pay $3 and everyone else pays $15 for two bags.

During the winter season the Good Food Club coordinator buys healthy food in bulk and distributes it by the 40-lb box each month to club members for a fraction of the price they would normally pay. The coordinator functions as a 'food organizer'. Who needs a food hamper when you can get a Good Food Box?

The Wolseley Family Place - Food Connections Project specializes in catering and healthy food education in their drop-in centre. With a full kitchen, the participants in the program learn how to prepare meals, are busy with catering commitments and are learning healthy alternatives to sugar-laden, packaged food. Their centre also operates a small store – selling products in small portions at affordable prices. As caterers, they are providing heart-smart muffins, snacks and full meals. This project is one of four groups that LITE employs to bake cookies and cakes for the holiday season for Cheer Board hampers.

LITE's most visible event is its annual Wild Blueberry Pancake Breakfast. Three community caterers, with groceries purchased from Neechi Foods, serve up pancakes and muffins to 800 breakfast guests. Sixteen local residents are employed, another 20 local CED initiatives are given a public forum to sell their art and crafts and the wider Winnipeg community can actively support this growing network of organizations building more sustainable communities – simply by eating pancakes! Ah, food. It really is fabulous.

LITE is committed to spreading the good stories of CED in Winnipeg's inner-city though workshops, newsletters, poster and media campaigns and public events. There truly are alternatives to the current global economic model (that excludes the vulnerable and benefits those who already have plenty). LITE wants to give people ways of supporting this alternative economic stream. Individuals, community centres, institutions and government – all have ways of participating in this very real form of community building. The more the people of Winnipeg give to LITE, the more support LITE can give to these projects. The more people practising CED principles in their personal and corporate experiences, the less LITE will have to fundraise. We will all be more secure if the most vulnerable in our communities can experience real food security.

If you are interested in supporting LITE or getting to know more about the projects it supports: LITE 204-942-8578 litepr@mts.net www.lite.mb.ce

*LITE has adopted these 11 Neechi CED principles/questions as their guide:

Do you buy local goods and services?
Do you re-invest your profits in the community?
Do you provide long-term jobs for community members?
Do you provide training to develop the skills of community members?
Is your business owned and controlled by community members?
How do you support a healthier and safer community?
How does your business promote a better environment?
How are you contributing to a more stable neighbourhood?
How do you promote human dignity and equality?
How do you support other community development efforts?

Healthy Living Program

by Gerry Pearson

Who are We?

The Healthy Living Program, located at St Matthew's Maryland Community Ministry in the West Central Community in Winnipeg, Manitoba, has been working toward increasing food security for the community since March 2001. The work started with funds from Health Canada - Population and Public Health Branch in the Diabetes Prevention Strategy. In March 2003 the program changed its name and focus from Diabetes Prevention to Healthy Living. This change reflects the work being done in the program to include the prevention of other chronic diseases, in addition to diabetes, with healthy eating (food security) and active living.

The Healthy Living Program is a joint partnership between four community organizations: Klinic Community Health Centre, St Matthew's Maryland Community Ministry, Spence Neighbourhood Association and Diocesan Urban Aboriginal Ministry. The work grew out of knowledge gained in working with the community and programs that had been initiated by volunteers and students but had not been able to continue due to lack of resources. The strengths of a partnership such as this are immense and include shared expertise and other resources.

A population health approach and capacity building are key components of the program.

All programs are subsidized. Childcare is provided for all programs except the special events, which are family oriented. All programs offer a unique approach to education and skill development. Many folks in the community have had negative experiences with formal learning and authority so the typical forms of education are a barrier to participation and learning.

The Community

The West Central Community is one of the poorest communities in Winnipeg. Sixty percent of households live below the Low Income Cut Off level compared to twenty-eight percent for Winnipeg as a whole. Twenty-two percent are unemployed and twenty-one percent have less than grade nine education. There is a high concentration of single-parent, female-led families. The neighbourhood is densely populated. Sixty-one percent live in rental accommodation which is badly deteriorated. The neighbourhood is ethnically diverse, with twenty-two percent Aboriginal people and thirty-seven percent from Asia and Latin America.

The Programs

"Food to Go"- our version of Community Kitchen.

Food to Go addresses the accessibility (effective distribution) and acceptability (nutritionally adequate) aspects of food security. A small group of people cook a meal together and then take that meal home for their families. Everyone is involved in selecting the recipes, the cooking and the clean-up. Sharing experience and ideas is encouraged. Basic nutrition information and skills are taught in an informal way. The great things about Food to Go are the food and the connections people make with each other. Food to Go gives people a chance to try recipes they wouldn't try at home because they wouldn't risk its not turning out, they don't have the recipe or some ingredient, or they are unsure they have the skill to do it.

Program participants always get more variety than they would if they cooked at home on their own. The time and the energy required are reduced when people work together. Energy is something many people in the community lack. A small group of people working together can make quite a spread in a pretty short time!

Making sure the participants have an enjoyable experience cooking is very important. Laughter and caring are central to each cooking session. As people get to know each other, the sharing deepens. Some very moving moments have happened during Food to Go sessions. Moms have shared their fears about not being a "good mom," others have shared a diagnosis of cancer or depression and others have revealed pieces of just how difficult it is to live in poverty. Food to Go is also a place for folks to share celebrations such as a birthday, finding an apartment or quitting smoking. When you know that others care, it is easier to make the effort to come and cook.

As program coordinator, I have a better appreciation of how close to crisis people who live in poverty are all the time. Housing, safety, keeping your children and keeping them happy all take priority over eating, especially eating well. Lots of times, women, in particular, do not have much control over whether they will be able to participate in a program. A partner, a child, a parent or a distant relative's needs all have the power to pull a woman out of a cooking program.

Many people in the community have lots of knowledge about diabetes and what it would take to be able to be healthy. Many also have lots of skill and capacity to run the program independent of outside assistance. It is the fragility of living in poverty that keeps that from happening.

Lunch Program for JobWorks Youth Builders

This is a lunch program at an organization in the community that offers academic upgrading and employment preparation through carpentry. The participants are men and women between the ages of 16 and 29. Once a week, the Healthy Living Coordinator and two community volunteers work with the participants to create a lunch for the entire group. Participants take turns making lunch. The staff tell us that the best attendance in the program is "lunch day." The objectives are for the participants to experience what it is like to eat a healthy lunch while they are working, learn how to make a healthy, low-cost bag lunch and learn the importance of eating well. What is great about this program is although youth is a difficult group of people to attract to programs, when the lunch program is part of their program, they participate and gain valuable experience and knowledge.

One of the greatest things about this program is the involvement of community volunteers as assistants and positive role models in the program. The community volunteers bring experience and knowledge that the current coordinator could not offer, such as Aboriginal culture and parenting. Many of these young people either have or will soon be starting a family of their own. They are making the transition to becoming adults responsible for feeding and caring for their own children. Parenting is a great motivation to learn about eating well and being physically active. This program also addresses accessibility and acceptability– culturally acceptable and nutritionally adequate aspects of food security.

Special Events

"Eat more vegetables!" sounds boring, and is unattainable to many people but, "come out to an evening with healthy food and fun activities" sounds like something they wouldn't want to miss. This is the approach we take with all the special events–come and have fun, and, by the way, you are eating nutritious food and being physically active. Special events such as the annual

Scavenger Hunt, in all its versions, the Mystery Dinner Theatre, the Travelling Dinner and Community Feast are about eating well, being active and building community.

The great things about the events are they attract people who may not be involved in any other program or organization, everyone has fun, the food is delicious and it is a celebration of our community. The Community Garden Preserves group at St Matthew's Maryland Community Ministry, a small group of community members, always cater to the events. Each group member earns a small honorarium, and equally important, each person takes pride in offering their work to the community.

The special events are a big hit in the community. People are looking for ways to have fun. The events help people put aside their worries, including what is for dinner, for an evening or a Saturday morning. The events are something to look forward to, even if the next one is six months away. The stories from the events circulate all through the year.

This program also addresses the accessibility and acceptability aspects of food security.

Kids in the Kitchen

St Matthew's Maryland Community Ministry has been fortunate to receive money to hire students as Urban Green Team members for a number of summers. The Green Team is responsible for the children's program and for the past three years we have worked together to have a "Kids in the Kitchen" component to the program. The program is for 5-to 12-year-olds. Each year we have a theme for the kitchen program, such as making the connection between the garden and what we grow with what we eat. The program involves making something in the kitchen, some physical activities and a craft that are all related to the theme.

What is great about the program is the enthusiasm the children have in the kitchen. Some children don't have much experience in the

kitchen and so love the chance to "make it themselves"! We get an opportunity to have them make and eat a healthy snack and we provide some teaching with that as well.

What we have learned is that it takes a high ratio of adults to children to make the experience enjoyable for everyone. Attention spans are quite short and so we need lots of different activities each time. The children love the program. We have used Kids in the Kitchen, Manitoba Milk Producers, Youville Clinic, Heart and Stroke Foundation, First Nations and Inuit Health Branch, Health Canada The Winnipeg Regional Health Authority and The Tickle Trunk (Manitoba Association of Community Health) as resources.

Think and Do Game

This game helps people use and share their creative thinking to solve common problems faced in making food choices and in trying to meet their own and their family's nutritional requirements. This is a board game that was modified to focus on diabetes prevention and healthy living in general. The players land on "think" or "do" squares, they pick up a card from that pile, and using, their option cards, either answer the question themselves, ask someone else to help them answer the question, ask the whole group the question or pass. The questions are "what do you think…" or "what would you do" and so do not have one correct answer. Of course, some answers are better than others and this is the beauty of the game because other players can offer their ideas too. The questions are about problem solving in order to be healthier. The questions spark creativity. Examples of food-related questions in the family version of the game are: "Molly and Golly, two cows from Minnedosa, have sent you some milk. They want to know how many different things you could make with their milk. What are they?" "Your mom wants you to try to eat food that you have never eaten before. It is not always easy. What do you think would make it easier to try new food?"

The great things about the game are that people like to share their ideas and help others. The questions often make people laugh while they think about a serious problem. Everyone wins and everyone helps each other out. All ideas are honoured and respected. When we played this game with children, we worked in teams and we created a taped version of the board on the floor. Each team physically moved on the board instead of using a material marker.

Ready-Made Entrée Program

This is a pilot program from January 2005 to March 31, 2005. The goal of the program is to provide nutritionally dense entrées to community folks who are most vulnerable to eating poorly. These are people who live alone, may be depressed, have substance abuse issues or have other physical or mental health issues. They have difficulty shopping and cooking for themselves and often roam from a drop-in, to a soup kitchen, to a relative's home to address their hunger. They lack hot, home-cooked meals that are nutritionally balanced. This pilot period will give us an opportunity to determine if participants feel healthier or more energized after eating the entrée, if they feel more motivated to cook for themselves or eat more balanced meals, and if they learn anything about nutrition through the program. It will also give us an opportunity to determine if this program could prepare people for participation in the Food to Go program. The meals are a crucial part of the program but equally important are the relationships made between staff and participants. It is hoped that staff can help participants access other community resources that may benefit their overall health.

One of the good things about this program is that the Community Garden Preserves group (a small group of community members at St. Matthew's Maryland Community Ministry) are doing the meal preparation and helping with the meal planning and distribution.

We are looking forward to providing some concrete food security to people who are in most need of nutritious food, and to learning more about what would assist them to eat better.

Conclusion

The Healthy Living Program in the West Central Community of Winnipeg offers a variety of opportunities to access food, learn some basic nutrition information, develop basic skills and build community. The community is very positive about the program and many people have come to look forward to and rely on the food and social support. The program builds as community involvement increases and as we learn what engages the community. The unfortunate piece is the funding is not secure. We have been fortunate to have funds for three years but are currently in a position of having less than one year's funding secured. Much time and effort go into trying to find funds. Program costs are minimal with one paid staff, many volunteers and shared resources.

The Stop Community Food Centre

The Community Food Centre:
Building Community, a Healthy
Environment and Social Justice
Through Food
by Charles Z Levkoe with
Rhonda Teitel-Payne and Nick Saul

The Stop Community Food Centre
is a Toronto-based, grassroots, non-profit
organization that is working to widen its
approach to issues of food insecurity by
combining direct service with capacity
building and sustainable community
development. The Stop works primarily
with vulnerable populations in Davenport
West, an area that has been identified as
one of the poorest and most under-serviced
in Toronto. This is largely due to stagnant
and decreasing incomes (social assistance
rates that don't reflect the cost of living,
a low minimum wage and a loss of well-
paying jobs) and increasing costs (high
rents and rising food prices). Given this
context, it's not surprising that thousands
of people in our community struggle to
put food on their table each day.

The Stop originally opened in the late
1970s at the St. Stephen-in-the-Fields
Church in downtown Toronto, distributing
food to people living on low incomes. In
1985, once the food bank was well
established, The Stop became
involved with advocacy work

in the form of assisting people with
landlord-tenant disputes and welfare and
unemployment problems. As The Stop
evolved, two, central, interconnecting
ideologies led its work. The first was that
confronting hunger must go beyond
handing out food to people struggling
on low incomes. The second is that
food access and food security are basic
human rights.

Over the last six years The Stop has
developed a new service-delivery model
that moves beyond food banks as the
only response to hunger and poverty. We
call our model a Community Food Centre
(CFC). At the heart of this project is the
promotion of food security. This refers to
a strategy where all people, regardless of
gender, race or social class, have access to
adequate amounts of safe, nutritious and
culturally appropriate food produced in
an environmentally sustainable way and
provided in a manner that promotes
human dignity.

Traditionally, hunger has been viewed
as an issue of charity. The Stop is
working hard to reveal the systemic
causes of food insecurity that marginalize
certain individuals and groups through
community development and food access
programming. Many personal accounts
show that passively receiving food is not
only demeaning to recipients but also
perpetuates structural inequality. When
people become actively involved in
creating solutions to food insecurity in
their community, they feel less stigmatized.
They also develop their skills further, feel
less isolated, build support networks and
learn how to have a greater influence in
making change.

The Stop's unique perspective brings
together a number of approaches in
the field of food security, melding
respectful emergency food delivery with
community development, social justice
and environmental sustainability. Most
organizations working on food issues tend
to focus their efforts on one aspect of
food security, whereas The Stop attempts
to take a wider approach.

The Stop's programs include a food bank, a number of community gardens, an environmental and food-security education initiative, The Stop café, community kitchens, an outdoor bake oven, drop-in programs, perinatal nutrition and support, civic engagement and various other community development initiatives.

The Stop has moved towards this model over the years in fitful leaps and bounds, creating new programs and policies and sharing its successes to the best of its ability with limited resources. There are a number of factors at work that are necessary for The Stop to function as a Community Food Centre. These include a clear understanding of the local needs and assets within its community, a progressive and well-communicated vision, the ability to take risks by implementing and working with new ideas, a democratic working environment that includes the skills and knowledge of staff and a participatory planning approach that encourages interactive decision making with community members. The strength of the Community Food Centre model is that it does not depend on only one individual to take responsibility. A diverse staff team, an active board and engaged community have been key contributors to its evolution.

In order to ensure our work reflects and responds to the needs of our community, The Stop has developed a number of methods of participatory feedback and communication (i.e. town halls, community planning dinners). Community members are first connected to the organization through direct programming, but over time become more deeply engaged with food issues through popular education, participatory activities and advocacy. This helps to break down the stigma and humiliation often associated with asking for help with food and creates responses that offer dignity, not just a handout.

Since the establishment of our Community Food Centre we have compiled evidence of the impact of our services primarily through observation and experience. Program logs and records have shown a dramatic increase in the numbers of people participating in

The Stop's programs and confirmed that people want to be active participants (as cooks, gardeners, volunteers and engaged citizens) in dealing with their food concerns. Also, the development of new programs consistently brings in a new range of people who have never used The Stop before. For example, the establishment of a drop-in brought in more homeless men and new Spanish-speaking people began attending once we offered a community kitchen program in their language. Another important piece of evidence has been the positive reputation of The Stop among community members and social service organizations in the city and across the country.

The Stop's newest initiative, The Green Barn, exemplifies its leadership role and progressive reputation in the community. The project, which is part of a larger development, will see The Stop managing a greenhouse, sheltered gardens, an outdoor bake oven and food systems education programs at an old Toronto Transit Commission site in the City of Toronto. The Green Barn will embody in a very tangible way The Stop's holistic approach to food security and its success is critical to the long-term health of the organization.

For more information about The Stop Community Food Centre, please check out its Web site at www.thestop.org.

Project : A Day to Fulfill our Biggest Dream

1. Food Bank Component

To meet the needs of community-based agencies by collecting, processing and freely distributing quality food, namely through emergency food services, in support of their social development mission for the needy population of the Greater Montréal area and other regions in the province.

2. Sustainable Development Component

To help the agencies being served find and develop long-term solutions to the problems their mission seeks to respond to, by networking agencies, providing training through the pooling of experience, and ensuring the active participation of the appropriate authorities for local, regional and national joint efforts.

3. Advocacy Component

To provide leadership by exercising its influence to defend, promote and develop food security with the general public and with private and public authorities, in solidarity and partnership with the social movement for the war against poverty.

Each week, some 50 volunteers assist Moisson Montréal in administration, food sorting and maintenance. The volunteers generally stem from disadvantaged circles or are looking for experience to integrate into Québec society. The food bank also has volunteers for special events such as the media's Grande Guignolée. These volunteers are drawn from the general public and from business. Despite all this, there are not enough volunteers to carry out all the tasks required keep the food bank running smoothly. In order to ensure the quality of the food being distributed to community-based agencies, more volunteers are needed to sort the incoming food.

Project: A Day to Fulfill Our Biggest Dream

Ever since it was created in 1984, Moisson Montréal has been dreaming of redistributing top-quality products to its agencies, out of respect for the dignity of the recipients of these goods. However, 60% of the food collected has to be sorted to separate the edible products from those that are damaged.

Projet: Une grand reve en 1 journee
by Marie-Noëlle DeVito

Moisson Montréal in a Nutshell

In 2004-2005, Moisson Montréal distributed 9.5 million kilograms of food and essentials to more than 225 community agencies being served directly and indirectly and to 16 other regional food banks in Québec. Each month in the Greater Montréal area, more than 150,000 people in distress, including 65,000 children, are able to profit from the help of Moisson Montréal.

For the past ten years, Moisson Montréal has given itself the mandate to coordinate, in its warehouses, national food sharing for Québec and the Maritimes (CAFB). Also, since 2004, it has been on AQBAM's permanent committee for national and provincial food sharing. Thus, thanks to its judicious management of national and provincial food sharing, it reaches more than 350,000 people through 16 other food banks in the province.

Moisson Montréal distributes 60,000 kilograms of food every day.

Overall Mission

Moisson Montréal is committed to striving for the food security of the destitute in the Greater Montréal area, in partnership with the community, and champions developing long-term solutions to poverty-related issues.

Ever-increasing needs and the lack of regular volunteers prevent Moisson Montréal from reaching one of its goals, which is to distribute a greater quantity of top-quality products every day. The shortage of volunteer workers makes this goal difficult to achieve on a daily basis.

In order to be in a position to offer greater amounts of sorted food items, Moisson Montréal has developed a project called A Day to Fulfill Our Biggest Dream. The idea is quite simple: 1 agency, 10 volunteers, 1 day a year. Given that Moisson Montréal distributes food to more than 225 agencies, if each one of them donated one day of volunteer work to come and sort the food, it would benefit the entire network of agencies and the people they serve all year long.

The people targeted by this project are the salaried workers, volunteers and administrators of every agency likely to be involved in this solidarity activity.

Here is what a typical day looks like for the A Day to Fulfill Our Biggest Dream project:

8:25 a.m.	Welcome
8:30 a.m.	Tour of Moisson Montréal
8:45 a.m.	Arrival at the sorting centre. The day's task is explained
10:00 a.m.	Break (15 min.)
11:30 a.m	Lunch (60 min.)
2:30 p.m.	Sorting ends and clean up of sorting tables begins
3:00 p.m.	The agency leaves

That is the schedule for a typical day. However, it is subject to change, depending on the food collected, since Moisson Montréal has no way of knowing what the daily shipments will contain. Leaving times may vary, but will never be later than 3:00 p.m.

Positive Aspects of The A Day to Fulfill Our Biggest Dream Project

By taking part in this initiative, agencies make it possible to:

• Improve the quality of the food distributed to all agencies;

• Reduce the volume of inedible food distributed to agencies;

• Reduce the resources agencies need to assign to the sorting of food;

• Heighten their visibility and be given an exemplary citation for their social involvement, management and autonomy;

• Take part in a fantastic day of sharing in the big food aid chain.

The A Day to Fulfill Our Biggest Dream project is a wonderful opportunity to strengthen the partnerships developed between Moisson Montréal and its recipient agencies. It is also a chance to make the best use of the human resources needed to operate the food bank well. Lastly, it makes it possible to multiply our actions for the people who benefit from the work we all do.

Outcome

Although participation in this project is voluntary, agencies have responded well to Moisson Montréal's call. From the very outset, in 2000-2001, some fifty agencies agreed to take part by donating a day of volunteer work. For the second year of the project, in 2001-2002, Moisson Montréal took in 400 volunteers from various agencies who donated almost 2000 hours. Lastly, in 2002-2003, more than 350 people from some fifty agencies put in 1500 hours of volunteer work.

To sum up, the A Day to Fulfill Our Biggest Dream project has made it possible to improve the quality of products being distributed, make the operations of the food bank better known to the groups being served, and increase the exchanges between community-based agencies and Moisson Montréal.

Community-Academic Research Partnership

A Key Recipe for Food Security
by Connie Nelson, Margaret Stadey,
and Ariel-Ann Lyons

Science is sceptical. Community action is idealistic…. We need to nurture the drive for fundamental new understanding of social and community processes at the same time that we engage in action for community development and change (Price & Behrens, 2003).

Our experiences suggest that a community-academic research partnership is a key food security recipe to bring to the table. Our premise for this partnership is that the research knowledge gained helps the community build confidence to act on food security issues. This confidence for action arises because in the process of building a partnership, we strengthen trusting relationships, increase the density of social networks and share community norms and sanctions (Kawachi, et al., 1999; Coleman, 1988; Freudenberg, 1986). This builds collective efficacy (Morenoff et al., 2001; Sampson, et al., 1999; & Sampson, et al., 1977) whereby a community understands and engages in actions that demonstrate the shared belief that food insecurity is a drag on the well-being of both individuals and the community as a whole.

This community-academic research partnership is a long-term commitment that in less than two years has already achieved many successes, and in doing so has built new networks, solidified others and developed a trusting commitment among many people to achieve both a greater awareness of food insecurity issues and to enhance the level of food security in the community.

This partnership is ongoing and so a selected number of the successful initiatives are briefly explained, followed by a list of the recipe ingredients and directions for others to follow in developing a community-academic research partnership.

Examples of Outcomes of the Community-Academic Research Partnership Recipe

Many of the research activities in this partnership overlap and have developed in a non-linear fashion that seized on 'just-in-time' opportunities. This includes unique strengths and interests of individuals and available resources to further the local knowledge base on food security. These examples are not an exhaustive list but are to serve as catalysts for ideas as to how others may use our recipe to develop their own specific research outcomes. First, over an 18-month period, 35 emergency food distribution services came together to work with the academic partner in developing a survey to analyze the relationship between food needs and the extent of social challenges experienced among people who access emergency food services in Thunder Bay and surrounding communities.

Factors considered included job loss, high tuition, low fixed income, high housing costs or any other reasons that lead to food insecurity. Fourth-year undergraduate students enrolled in a research methodology course distributed the survey. The words of the students, future social workers who will be interfacing directly with persons seeking help and who have food security issues, best epitomizes some of the immediate outcomes of this partnership.

Dr. Nelson allowed us to participate in a Food Distribution Survey where we interviewed people in the community who attend food banks in Thunder Bay. In doing so, she allowed us to gain valuable hands-on experience in the field, experience a unique understanding of the research process and illustrate how important it is to connect people and the concept of research.

By visiting food banks throughout Thunder Bay and the surrounding district, we realized how important our role as social workers is in advocating for people who cannot speak for themselves. We heard first-hand stories of how the system has failed people within the community, an experience that will be forever engrained in my mind and inspire me to do better.

On a daily basis, I am impacted by the lack of food resources for my clients. I think about the study we did, the people we met and how the impact of food insecurity is tenfold. Without food, what else can a person accomplish?

Another outcome is a clearer understanding locally that emergency food services are a necessary band-aid for systemic issues of the working poor and of inadequate social assistance. More to the point, the community has acquired evidence-based knowledge to guide efforts to look beyond emergency food needs to broader food security issues.

The face-to-face distribution of these surveys gave the participants a chance to convey first-hand their support for the research. Many of these participants suggested that the survey was too narrow and that they wanted to enhance our understanding with more in-depth stories of how they deal with food security. Building on this feedback, students are now carrying out a phenomenological study focussing on the broader issues of what happens to people and families coping with food security concerns. This study, while not completed, is raising awareness about how emergency food distribution programs can reduce the person to the status of 'victim' of the problem. In the words of one of the participants, "I think of our discussion at the Client Advisory meeting last fall when we decided that this type of research was needed. We were talking about the social stereotype that we as people were being defined by. It allows society to treat the victim as the one who needs help instead of the system that endorses the abuse or the poverty or the food need. I haven't lost my fight – and many others are also unwilling to give up their humanness to the political will. I think that others have been made to feel ashamed of their failure to measure up – being deemed 'a waste of skin' by those who would judge them unworthy of consideration." The participant then offered this advice to the student researchers: "Pay attention for little things – pain is not always spoken of with tears and remember that the pain can be very deep." Further, as a result of a class discussion, the graduate assistant for the course added these insights to help the students understand what they are observing and experiencing in this phenomenological study.

I had a thought about today's class. There seemed to be a theme around research partners avoiding discussing their food needs. Here is a possible hypotheses as to why that may be: over the last decade or more, those living in poverty have been presented in a very negative light by the dominant narrative. This social construction of the poor creates an environment in which the mistreatment of our fellow citizens, both adults and children, can be seen by the public as the right thing to do. We are all influenced by this constant stream of messages, which influences how we perceive poverty and what it is to be poor—none of us lives in a vacuum. This includes your research partners who also receive these same messages. They are also told that being poor and all things associated with poverty are negative, which would include themselves and the people they love. The message they also constantly receive is: to be good. they must be something other then who they happen to be—they must be more like those who have judged them inadequate—they must present those attributes that others have deemed of value.

Have no illusions about this: to challenge the dominant narrative of self internally or externally no easy task for you or your research partners. So, maybe what these people are trying to tell you with their discussions about other things is: 'please believe me, I am a good person.'

The intended long-term outcome of this study is to give voice to food security issues so that those who experience them and those who are in policy positions can more closely align solutions.

Another completed outcome was a graduate research phenomenological study to explore how community gardening experiences can affect perceptions of self-sufficiency, quality of life and level of food security. This study showed that people who must use emergency food resources seemed to have very little control over their lives. They are forced to deal with the survival issues necissitated by not having enough money or resources to acquire basic needs. The current social policies adopted by the government and other funding bodies contribute to this lack of control and power, and can inhibit a move away from a life of poverty. Study findings suggest that this powerlessness and lack of control are transferred to activities that are meant to improve self-sufficiency, such as community gardening. Thus, the community has learned that for community gardens to be successful, there must be a focus on the underlying systemic issues that drive food insecurity (Kerr, 2004).

In addition, one graduate and two undergraduate field practicums have helped to promote self-sufficiency through gardening, helped establish a new and vibrant food distribution association, helped rejuvenate participation in the local national Hunger Count and assisted in building Geographic Information System (GIS) maps locating emergency food programs in relation to community resources and socio-economic characteristics. All these efforts have helped to establish trusting relationships, strengthened shared community norms and enhanced the density of community networks in food security.

Ingredients for the Community-Academic Research Partnership Recipe

• The Contextual Fluidity model of practice contains five essential characteristics that guide the recipe for the community-academic partnership model, (Nelson & McPherson 2004; 2003). The partnership embraces a fluid process that focusses on building resilience, robustness, diversity and ductility. This fluid process assumes life contains its vicissitudes and simply accepts this. Formal and informal interactions occur within dynamic and ever-changing webs of networks that have no designated centre. Instead, these interactions are grounded within context.

• The anchor remains the vision. In this case, our belief is that "food security exists when every member of the community can with dignity put food on their own table." The contextual space-time is in constant motion as network interactions receive, relay and interpret information through both formal and informal linkages. Thus, the Contextual Fluidity practice model endorses the 'strange attractors' of formal and informal, planned and unplanned, and conscious and unconscious interactions in distinct and at times distant parts of the partnership.

• Community-capacity building principles include focus on vision as a driving force for action, the strength of multiple relationships, build shared values, the importance of participation in the process, a keen ear for listening to all community voices, be an insider engaging as a community member, focus on strengths, not problems, be opportunistic in using a diversity of resources, find ways to respect and bring out the unique gifts of individuals and groups, put more energy into the process than into definitive plans, accept and build from mistakes, and engage all (Nelson & Stadey, 2004a, 2004b).

Recipe Directions:
Stir the Following.

• Begin with one committed member of the academic system and one committed member from the community system who share a way of being, doing and practising their skills.

• Bring the two together in a common concern for the larger community to which they both belong.

• Involve them in a vision shared by others that can be assisted in its achievement by a community-academic partnership.

• Open up the opportunity and extend the invitation to others to participate within both the academic and community context.

• Blend gently and purposefully with the Contextual Fluidity model of practice.

• Add a sprinkle of all the interactions, with liberal portions of the principles of community capacity building. This empowers the many individual participants to be still or move as they see fit and to take their place in the community-building process. At the same time, it allows the networks to ripple, expand, grow, overlap, dissolve, regroup and start over as needed, while the multi-partnerships move through the process.

• Respect the pace that best serves the collective movement toward fulfilling the desired outcome as set by the company of participants.

• Garnish the interactions with understanding, patience and compassion; with smiles, friendship and laughter; with tolerance, strength and trust.

• Serve generous helpings of celebration as steps are accomplished to encourage and nurture continued efforts toward the common goal.

With nurture and dedication, science and community action can be united to produce extraordinary outcomes, as we have experienced in our community. In order to establish food-secure communities, we must understand social and community processes to create fundamental change. Use our ingredients and follow our directions to create a community-academic partnership in your community. We feel confident that you will be delighted and engaged with both expected and unexpected benefits of this process.

References

Coleman, J. (1988) Social capital in the creation of human capital. *American Journal of Sociology*, 94, 95-120.

Freudenberg, W.R. (1986). The density of acquaintanceship: An overlooked variable in community research? *American Journal of Sociology*, 92(1), 27-63.

Kerr, H. (2004). Community building: A case study of emergency food need users and the development of self-sufficiency in community gardening. Unpublished master's research project, Lakehead University, Thunder Bay, Ontario, Canada.

Kawachi, I., Kennedy, B.P., Glass, R. (1999). Social capital and self-rated health: A contextual analysis. *American Journal of Public Health*, 89(8), 1197-1193.

Morenoff, J.D., Sampson, R.J., Raudenbush, S.W. (2001). Neighborhood inequality, collective efficacy, and the spatial dynamics of urban violence. *Criminology*, 39(3), 517-559.

Nelson, C.H. & McPherson, D.H. (2004). Contextual fluidity: An emerging practice model for helping. *Rural Social Work*, 9, 199-209.

Nelson, C.H. & McPherson, D.H. (2003). Cultural diversity in social work practice: where are we now and what are the challenges in addressing issues of injustice and oppression? In Wes Shera (Ed.), *Emerging perspectives on anti-oppressive practice* (pp. 81-100). Toronto: Canadian Scholars Press.

Nelson, C. H., & Stadey, M. (2004, May 29a). The confluence of food security and nutritional and mental health well-being: A transformative partnership. Invited Plenary Presentation 2004 CASSW-ACESS Conference, Congress of the Humanities and Social Sciences. Winnipeg: Manitoba.

Nelson, C. H., & Stadey, M. (2004, May 30b). The transformative power of community. 2004 CASSW-ACESS Conference, Workshop. Congress of the Humanities and Social Sciences. Winnipeg: Manitoba.

Price, R.H. & Behrens, T. (2003). Working Pasteur's quadrant: Harnessing science an action for community change. *American Journal of Community Psychology*. 31(3/4). 219-223.

Sampson, ,R.J., Morenoff, J.S. & Earls, F. (1999). Beyond social capital: Spatial dynamics of collective efficacy for children. *American Sociological Review*, 64(5), 633-660.

Sampson, R.J., Raudenbush, S.W. & Earls, F. (1997). Neighborhoods and violent crime: A multilevel study of collective efficacy. *Science*, 277(5328), 918-924).

What does Poverty Look Like to You?
by Basha Rahn

On behalf of the Child Poverty Action Committee and the Social Planning Advisory Network of Williams Lake, British Columbia.

The Child Poverty Action Committee (CPAC) is a sub-committee of the Social Planning Advisory Network (SPAN) of Williams Lake and has been active since 1996. Spurred by the 1989 federal and provincial campaigns to eliminate child poverty by the year 2000 and by the fact that child poverty instead increased to 1.4 million Canadian children by the year 2000, CPAC works to raise awareness of poverty in our community, to broaden perspectives about poverty and for social change.

We are a mixture of people and their experiences. We are:

• People who are living in poverty
• People who have lived in poverty
• People who don't live in poverty but are concerned with the issues

CPAC held its 4th Poverty Challenge in February 2005. This event takes participants through a variety of tasks that simulate the physical/emotional challenges that low-income families face everyday.

Real-life scenarios are written and participants are invited from the community to experience first-hand, for one day, the barriers that many families struggle with every day. The challenge illustrates the complexity of food security and its impact on health. The Poverty Challenge aims to raise awareness and challenges a variety of stakeholders to better understand the issues.

The Poverty Challenges will be used as a model to develop a capacity-building manual for food security and poverty. The manual was developed in March 2005 from funding received from Interior Health, British Columbia, to increase awareness of food security issues and address changes that may have an impact, the social determinants of health. This how-to resource will illustrate the insights and feedback from the participants' perspectives, as each lives through his or her scenario for one day. This unique event also creates an opportunity for participants to revisit their own beliefs and assumptions about living in poverty. This tool, which illustrates the benefits of collaboration on food security issues, within a community, can be utilized to challenge the long standing opinions or perspectives many people express about those who live in poverty. It can create social change.

Make Gardening History

by Wayne Roberts

There's more to food than meets the stomach, which explains why leaders of Botswana's campaign for AIDS prevention made a return visit to Toronto.

A delegation of Botswana city health officials came to Toronto about 18 months ago, and went home to set up a good food box program for homecare patients with AIDS based on FoodShare Toronto's signature program (itself borrowed from Brazil some ten years ago), and community gardens similar to those provided in Toronto parks. Last month, another delegation from Botswana – the country with the highest rates of HIV infection in the world, despite a variety of proactive government programs – came to check out how gardening programs could deliver education on safe sex and AIDS prevention to youth.

They thereby raised the stakes in the debate about food in anti-poverty and economic development groups. Food is no longer just a physical object that provides meals, nutrients and boosted immunity. It's a subject that provides education and empowerment. It's no longer just about a right to consume enough good food. It's also about a right to produce and be engaged.

The tour won't exactly "make poverty history" in keeping with last month's gala demonstrations for African economic development. But the venture to "make gardening history" may set the standard for community development programs that sink deep roots and deliver on the ground.

I've been asked to lead a tour of food-producing gardens by Barbara Emanuel of Toronto Public Health, who coordinates their partnership with health and city staff from southeast Botswana working on innovative approaches to AIDS prevention and treatment.

We start the day at Sunshine Garden, a 6000-square-foot plot of land on the treed and grassy grounds of the Centre for Addiction and Mental Health (CAMH) on Queen West in Parkdale. Like most of the successful garden experiments in Toronto, this is based on the social equivalent of companion planting, where species are snuggled up to each other so all can gain strength from the strong points of one – as in corn, which needs lots of nitrogen, serving as a pole for climbing beans, which draw down nitrogen from the air, while the broad leaves of squash provide ground cover that keeps the soil from drying up. Karine Jaouich manages this little oasis on behalf of FoodShare, which is companion planted with the United Way and CAMH to convert the garden into an employment readiness project that teaches work skills to mental health out-patients while creating some community feeling with local residents through a weekly farmers market that the gardeners supply. Food is a tool to break down institutional barriers and let people connect on their own to meet mutual and reciprocal needs, I pontificate.

That's actually right, Jaouich tells me, because of the way roles get reversed. CAMH clinicians and caseworkers get to see a side of patients they never see in formal setting, and garden workers training in this multicultural plot of land get to guide and help medics and social workers who wouldn't know a snake gourd from an okra plant, or that a luffa is an edible vegetable, not just a harsh sponge for the shower.

It's about basing therapeutic relationships on talents and gifts, not just needs, I pontificate again.

Garden variety work lets abilities, not disabilities, come to the fore, says Jaouich. Some jobs are perfect for someone with a bad back, need to vent energy or desire to focus and concentrate in silence, she says. "There are so many things to do, it's just a matter of mixing and matching the right skill to the right job." There are even raised containers that can be worked by people in wheelchairs or with bad backs, the kinds of adaptations that are crucial when gardeners are weakened by AIDS.

The downtime from rainy days also has its up-side. That's when the gardeners have their lifeskills workshops on shopping, cooking, hygiene and the like. Aha, so time for outreach work and teaching does get folded in, the Botswana visitors understand. The time for the talk on personal hygiene is when the food is being prepared for sale, not when the lesson plan says so. Gardening is sprinkled with teachable moments, I pontificate again.

Of 146 people who've worked on this garden and job readiness project over four years, only nine have been readmitted to the CAMH hospital. That's a success rate few psychiatric facilities can match.

Then we're off to The Stop Community Food Centre at Davenport, at the centre of the third-highest need area in the city. It's called a community centre, and it is. People who use the food bank or emergency meal programs are members, not clients, have a vote at the stop meetings and are served as if they've come to a restaurant. This approach is crucial when working to overcome the stigma associated with poverty or AIDS, Barb Emanuel notes.

Our guide is Charles Levkoe, who coordinates 70 volunteers helping with The Stop's urban agriculture programs. The garden across from the centre is being worked by kids under ten, filling in the arts and crafts period of their day. "We can do arts and crafts, we can do gameshows, we can do running around, we can do environmental education," says Levkoe.

"An outdoor classroom is a perfect classroom."

Then we're off to the FoodShare warehouse in the abandoned industrial district in the south of the city, where we're treated to a stir-fry featuring tofu, which our guests from Botswana, where cattle and meat are plentiful, have never tasted. "The easiest mistake to make with Africa is to make general assumptions," Esau Mbanga, a lead manager in the southeast district, tells me.

Zahra Parvinian, manager of 14 youth paid to gain employment readiness and life skills in FoodShare's potpourri of beehives, composting, rooftop gardening, seedlings and foodbox loading, is our tour guide. A social worker, she has Dineo Segabai, the social worker in charge of southern Botswana's youth work and orphan care (orphans are a common legacy of AIDS in Africa), hanging onto every word of her fellow professional.

Food is ideal for working with youth, Zahra says, because "from food comes love and care, and we learn respect, not just for something we put in our stomach, but for farmers and others who produce it." Without the teachable moments associated with food, "working with youth would be much harder," she says. Over many years of operating programs for at-risk and street-involved youth with funding from the federal government, FoodShare boats a 70% success rate of getting them back to school and family or on to jobs and housing.

Then it's off to the Rockliffe yards in the northwest of the city, a works yard with an old greenhouse that serves as a base in the summer for 200 junior gardeners under 12, who are called greenhouse technicians. Master gardener Solomon Boye, one of the city's most successful workers with at-risk youth, is also based there. Gardens are perfect youth educators, he says with a Ghanaian accent that gives his words an echo. "There are natural laws we can't argue with, and then there are societal laws that many youth have trouble with. In the garden, it is not old people telling youth what to do, it is nature's relentless laws."

The land is talking to us. If you don't water and care for this plant, it will die. It's a way for youth to work through these kinds of issues."

By this time, nature's laws had worked on us. It had been à long, hot day, and, not being a gardener, I hadn't planned for information overload. Our guests must get ready for upcoming tours of palliative care facilities and youth Internet cafes. Gardens take time and can't be rushed. Nor can too much be crammed into one space at one time. I'll have to wait to see what grows out of this, and gain a gardener's patience and inner calm, which is why gardening is good for youth and elder work, I pontificate to myself.

Hunger in Our Community

*Renfrew Collingwood
Food Security Initiative*
by Steve Andrews

The other day, Dave, a youth who infrequently comes to the youth drop-in centre, showed up. Dave (not his real name) is a quiet guy; he keeps his headphones on most of the time, looks at his shoes and has a kind of quirky sense of humour. He participates in some things, such as shooting hoops or using the computers, but, for the most part, is an outsider. If you take a good look at him, you will realize he is quite gaunt and not very clean. If you have a chat with him, you will notice his humour hides some mild disabilities and low self-esteem. In fact, he dropped out of school in grade ten.

Friday nights, along with the usual fun and games, we have a cooking program, called Kid's Kitchen. Some people upon observation, would call it a feeding frenzy. Nonetheless, the kids love to be part of it and volunteers love to lead it. And I've never met a teen who doesn't like to eat! I've often thought of it as nothing more than some fun and a chance to learn teamwork, resulting in a good snack.

Since then, I have learned otherwise on two different occasions. Last Friday, the volunteers who usually lead Kid's Kitchen, were unavailable. We decided, rather than run out to buy cooking ingredients, to skip it for the night.

We continued with other activities–floor-hockey, basketball, pool, computers, and games. However, throughout the evening, I heard from staff and volunteers that the kids were complaining that they were hungry. Unfortunately, no doubt thanks to my middle-class mindset, I reacted by saying, "They can go to Subway or get food when they go home." My teen is always hungry and given the chance would eat me out of house, home, and most of my paycheque. The next night, Saturday, we decided to go ahead with a preplanned summer's end BBQ, knowing we had plenty of hotdogs in the freezer. Well, we all know about plans and how they can go wrong. The hot dogs were gone. Stolen!

Some of us were angry. We'd had a lot of theft lately at Collingwood Neighbourhood House and many backpacks, skateboards, bikes and even our Play Station, controllers and all, had been stolen. We wanted to know who took the hotdogs and set out to find out. Some kids came forward to let us know that Dave had taken them. Well, if he did, we thought, that was just plain mean! The least he could have done is just taken one or two for himself. What did he do with the rest? Waste them! Talk about unfair to the rest of the kids!

One co-conspirator, who is often in trouble himself, told me that Dave actually took them home to his family. He knows, because he was with him. He described Dave's living conditions as abominable, with a family grateful for some food–no questions asked. This was not the first time I learned this about a youth at the Centre. Later, other kids who know Dave told us about how he lives and how desperate his circumstances are. So, there we were, listening to three or four of the most needy and often most ill-behaved youth in our community, describing the plight of a fellow youth with compassion, understanding and concern. They just ate chips for dinner that night, no hot dogs, without complaint.

It is Sunday now and as I write this article, I feel guilty. Not because I think I should or could feed the world, but because of my own reaction to the theft, that it was just another bad kid, causing problems in our community.

Can you imagine yourself so hungry that you would steal from others for your food? Can you imagine yourself turning a blind eye to your teen, doing it? I hope not. But there are many people in our community for whom this is a reality. Of course, none of us can individually feed the world. However, we can help local families and youth with the resources of the Neighbourhood House. Tomorrow, I will be on the phone trying to help Dave. Not all youth work is fun and games. I wish it were.

Will Dave have to pay back the hot dogs? Yes. Stealing is wrong and he and the other kids at the youth centre need to know there are consequences. We'll no doubt work out some form of restitution other than cash.

Earlier, I wrote that I had learned something. I learned that Dave wasn't mean-spirited and wasteful, just hungry, as was his family. I learned that for many of the kids who frequent the drop-in centre, the Friday night cooking is not just a fun snack: it is their meal. For some, the best one they get all week.

Most importantly, I learned, and keep relearning, even the toughest of kids in the toughest of circumstances can and do show compassion for those worse off than themselves. Too often we only see the worst youth have to offer, instead of the best!

It has been over a year since I wrote that article and I haven't seen Dave since. We have, however, in large part through the efforts of members of Renfrew Collingwood Food Security Institute (FSI), come a long way towards meeting food security challenges in our community.

In little over a year, the FSI has established education programs in gardening and harvesting and a breakfast program two mornings a week, and

plans are nearly complete for a community food-producing roof-top garden and community garden on the ground.

As a result of the FSI initiative, and a need being recognized to include youth in a meaningful way, we established Kid's Kitchen, a volunteer-led youth cooking/ dinner program on Friday nights.

A year ago we were cooking junk food for the youth on Friday nights. Now the food is healthy with the kids involved in all aspects – preparation, setup, eating and clean-up. Approximately 20 youth regularly prepare and cook healthy, well-balanced meals. That would make any health care professional smile. Better yet, they cook for approximately 20 other kids, who, though not interested in cooking, will eat for the price of helping with clean-up. Adults from our community, in particular Janice Kwan, one of the most devoted volunteers I have ever had the good fortune to work with, come in to our Neighbourhood House to cook healthy meals for, and most importantly with, our children.

This year we had the first ever Youth Drop-in Centre Christmas Dinner, and the youth also created two large Christmas hampers that were delivered to local families.

Kid's Kitchen has become more than just about food. It has become a lesson in healthy eating, in teamwork, in caring for others and in taking the time to sit and eat together.

At the same time, the local Health Centre (Evergreen) started a Teen Parenting & Pregnancy Program. Far more that just a clinic, this program, in partnership with Collingwood Neighbourhood House, tries to provide the education and supports necessary for these teenagers to become healthy, self-supporting, competent and caring parents. Many of these kids come from disadvantaged backgrounds, eat poorly at best and have had little experience in the family setting of a sit-down dinner.

Now, as part of the weekly program,
the youth, parents and parents-to-be,
and many newborns, sit down to a
healthy, well-balanced meal.

Yes, it's is about the food, but it's also about
community, respect and learning a family
tradition that has stood the test of time:
eating a meal together and sharing.

I look at how far we've come
and how far we have to go and
my hat goes off to those who have
committed themselves through the
Renfrew Collingwood Food Security
Institute and other organizations
to helping provide food, education
and ultimately self-sufficiency to
others in our community and to our
community's youth.

Take a Break

by Shefali Raja

Take a Break is a health education program that operates at the Trout Lake Community Centre in Vancouver, British Columbia, and has built a partnership with the Trout Lake Food Bank depot. The program started in July 1999 and operates weekly–except the week that welfare cheques are distributed. At the Trout Lake Food Bank depot, approximately 400 people line up for food. Of those 400, approximately 100 people drop in to Take a Break. Participants in the program include families, youth, singles and seniors on low income. Awareness of the program is thought to come largely from seeing it in operation and signs posted on the walls in four languages, English, Spanish, Vietnamese and Cantonese, in an attempt to increase peoples' access to the program.

The goal of Take a Break is to enable those families, children, youth, singles and seniors attending the food bank to improve their eating, health and well-being and to curtail hunger and malnourishment. The program is designed to accomplish this goal through four main objectives. The first is to alleviate immediate hunger needs and try to address the underlying causes of hunger. This is primarily done through the provision of healthy low-cost snacks that can be easily prepared and are appealing.

The second is to provide relevant and useful health education information that people can access. This is done by providing appropriate handouts and inviting discussion with the community health nurse and the community nutritionist. The third objective is to enable behaviour change regarding healthy food choices within their limited resources. This is done through teaching and modelling cooking skills. The cooking demos, educational material provided and discussions address the importance of the prevention of diseases such as diabetes, heart disease and obesity.

The fourth objective of the program is to help participants develop partnerships with other community-based initiatives or to develop awareness of other community- based services by inviting guest speakers to attend or providing information and pamphlets about these programs. Some of the community-based services include preschool programs, moms groups, ESL centres, social assistance, low-cost places to obtain food, cheaper dental facilities, youth clinics, neighbourhood houses, employee assistance programs, medical services or locating a physician, multicultural groups or mental health programs.

The program provides a relaxed, casual atmosphere staffed with a community health nurse and a community nutritionist as well as many volunteers. Take a Break also provides an opportunity for nutrition and nursing students to be involved in this community initiative by volunteering their time. It allows for valuable experience and exposure to community projects and increases awareness of programs that are available in the community.

Valuable activities are planned by the Take a Break coordinators in order to provide guidance, knowledge and awareness on key topics that affect families who are threatened by food insecurity. Participants in the program have an opportunity to taste a cooked dish that is healthy, tasty, easy to prepare and made using low-cost ingredients.

The prepared recipe is sometimes based on food items that are being distributed at the food bank that day, and often gives participants ideas on how to cook with food items with which they are unfamiliar. Written recipes are available for participants to take home to give families and singles new menu ideas and direction in the best buys for good nutrition while they are shopping. Recipes prepared most often use a wide variety of seasonal and affordable produce to promote increased fruit and vegetable consumption, as well as to introduce vegetables that may be unfamiliar to participants. The recipes are prepared to promote increased consumption of low-cost plant-based foods that also provide protein and iron, such as lentils, beans and tofu.

Food is a central component to Take a Break. Incorporating access to other information and community resources and empowering individuals are equally important to providing food in improving overall health and addressing the issue of food insecurity.

Regina Food for Learning

by Kay Yee

Mission Statement
Regina Food for Learning is a non-profit corporation formed to oversee the development and implementation of child food service programs in Regina schools and neighbourhoods. It is the largest child food service program in the city. Over the past 16 years we have offered programs in 25 locations and have served over 330,000 meals and 720,000 snacks to Regina schoolchildren.

History
Regina Food for Learning was incorporated in 1988 and began operating in April 1989. We started with a breakfast program at Core Ritchie for children from St. Augustine and Wetmore Schools. At that time Food for Learning was established by ordinary Regina citizens who were concerned about hungry children in our city. These people formed the volunteer base for the board of directors and breakfast program providers. There was no stable funding in place, and many of the groceries came from the food bank.

The Mayor's Task Force and the Regina Child Hunger Coalition weres in full swing and the City of Regina offered the half-time services of a city health department nutritionist for one year. She worked very closely with Food for Learning to set up menus, which were both nutritionally sound and economical. In fact, after her contracted services, she joined our Board of Directors as one of our strongest supporters.

The first year of operation was a real learning experience. We were very fortunate to have some very talented and committed people involved. We started with a breakfast program but soon realized that although breakfast is a very important meal each day, we would reach more children with a lunch program. We also found it easier to find the necessary volunteers at 9:00 a.m. instead of 7:00 a.m. The first year saw an expansion of services from one program to eight. Since then we have run ten programs at one time, and are currently providing lunches or snacks at ten locations.

Goals
• To provide children in low-income communities with nutritious food.

• To provide children with a role model that exemplifies good eating and nutritional habits.

• To encourage children to attend school with a positive outlook for the day.

• To develop a sense of community and camaraderie.

• To raise awareness of the issue of child hunger within the larger community.

• To generate financial support and volunteers for Regina Food for Learning.

Programs
We are presently providing lunches in seven locations and snacks in three locations. This means that we provide 663 children with 2495 snacks or lunches each week. All our programs are in response to a request from that particular school or community. We are reactive, not pro-active. It is our policy to not duplicate services in a location.

Nutritional Requirements

We were very fortunate to have the expertise of a nutritionist when we were first established. She set a high standard that we are still using. Each lunch provides one third of the nutritional requirements for the day. A typical lunch, consisting of four food groups, could be a meat, fish, egg, peanut butter or cheese sandwich, vegetable sticks, fruit or baked item and milk. A snack is made up of two food groups and could be crackers and cheese, fruit and a cookie, milk and a muffin, vegetable sticks and a hard-boiled egg, or one of the favourites–pizza buns.

Nutrition education is an important part of our program. Nutrition information is given to the children at every opportunity. We continually strive to introduce new foods whenever possible. There is an effort to provide as much variety as possible of fresh fruits and vegetables in season. It seems really hard to believe but when children at one of our locations were asked what fruit they thought they were eating four got it wrong before the fifth child identified fresh strawberries.

Volunteers and Staff

There are currently approximately 50 dedicated volunteers to whom we owe our success. These people are responsible for everything from lunch or snack preparation, grocery transportation, fundraising and cooking classes to being part of our volunteer board of directors.

We also have a paid staff of three part-time cooks, and a full time general manager to oversee all the programs, prepare menus, buy and distribute groceries and serve as the connecting link between the board of directors, volunteers, schools and cooks.

Funding

REACH is the umbrella organization, which oversees 14 feeding programs in the city.

Regina Food for Learning provided 21% of the meals and 44% of the snacks served by agencies under REACH in 2003/04.

Donations from individuals, service clubs, churches and businesses make up a good portion of our funding, while the balance is made up by different fundraising ventures. We are a registered charity and tax receipts are issued for amounts of ten dollars and over.

We pride ourselves in our money-management skills. Our costs are kept extremely low by a number of factors. Most importantly, our labour costs are minimal due to the dedication of our volunteers. We do not pay for office space, we work with a post office box address and the office itself is located in my home. Our food preparation and distribution locations are situated in City of Regina facilities or in the schools we serve. We are listed in the phone book under either Regina Food for Learning or Food for Learning and can be reached by fax or phone at (306) 565-8632. We also can be reached by email at rffl@accesscomm.ca or at our Website www.reginafoodforlearning.com.

Our menus and the grocery items we serve are first class. We purchase all our groceries very carefully. We do have what we call a "Wish List" of grocery items that we circulate to our donors. Some donors prefer to contribute food from the "Wish List." All in all, our efforts pay off as we have consistently kept our cost per lunch low – in 2004 it was $1.69. We feel this is quite an accomplishment for the nutritional value of each lunch. The cost includes all our expenses from the apples to the auditor.

Regina Food for Learning had a busy and productive year in 2004, serving 22,209 lunches and 67,150 snacks.

Mosque Meal

by Wayne Roberts

I had my first experience being part of a smiling jihad when I volunteered as an usher at a community meal put on by members of an east-Toronto mosque over the Easter weekend.

"Don't worry", Rashad ("call me Ray") said to me when he noticed I looked startled at the mention of jihad during the training session for volunteers, before doors opened to the public. Until then, I'd only heard the word in reference to some call to holy war by angry and harsh men referred to by the media as Islamic extremists. "Jihad is someone's first name," says Rashad, a college student in human resources. "It refers to effort or self-control." You can have a jihad to quit smoking, or a jihad to smile and be friendly when you're nervous that the people you're about to greet will be nervous about you, he said. "With a smile, you don't need to say much," operations coordinator Firaaz Azeez wraps up his pep talk to the ushers, greeters and hosts, reminding everyone to "struggle" to remain inviting and friendly and put guests at ease if anyone looks worried about their customs or intentions. "If someone eats and runs, we haven't done our job," he says. I struggle to learn my first lesson of the day in cross-cultural communication.

The jihad worked like a charm. The "hot soup day," as it's called, is directed to needy people across the city and to the Mosque's neighbours in Scarboro's Malvern neighborhood–commonly referred to as an at-risk neighbourhood facing problems of poverty, isolation and gangs. It's called a hot soup day so no one will think of it as a soup kitchen. And the cafeteria is decked out like a restaurant, complete with hosts, tablecloths, menu choices and waiters. About 800 people are served over the course of the day, but the pace is slow and easy. "It's the best I've ever been treated," says Randy, who bicycled here from half way across town after hearing about the offering at the meal program at his church. "If the whole world was run like this, we'd never have wars."

There's a whole lot of multiculturalism going on here. One level is between Muslim hosts and the largely non-Muslim guests. Another is among the Muslim hosts. I count about 30 nationalities among my fellow ushers, hosts and waiters, a legacy of the trade winds that blew seasonally along the east African coast and Arabian peninsula across to the Indian subcontinent, then Sri Lanka, Indonesia and Sumatra, trade winds that linked Islam to the highest achievements in astronomy, mathematics and science, centuries before Columbus sailed the ocean blue in 1492. When world power shifted from the Indian Ocean to the Atlantic, and Muslim areas became part of the colonized South, migrants in search of work in a global labour market took their faith to many other countries, most notably in the Caribbean. Though Arabic is used in prayers and religious sayings, as Latin was commonly used by Catholics on many continents, Islam is anything but a socially or culturally homogenous faith, let alone an Arabic one.

For new immigrants coming to a non-Muslim country like Canada inevitably makes the mosque a social as well as religious centre, says Salman Hasan, a Pakistani-born director of the Islamic Foundation of Toronto, because Muslims can no longer find educational and recreational services in the society-at-large, and so turn to their church to provide these services. "It's our job to be the custodian of the community," he says. But that didn't always mean that Toronto's many mosques worked together on social issues such as poverty or hunger, or looked to the Islamic Foundation to coordinate social efforts.

It's an ill tsunami that bears no good, and the giant wave that destroyed so many lives across southern Asia at Christmastime – striking Muslim populations in Indonesia and Sri Lanka most fiercely–unified Toronto's 350,000-strong Muslim community, the largest in North America, as few events could have done. On one day, six banquets raised over a million dollars and a Toronto-based medical team was sent to Indonesia.

The tsunami was a stark reminder of Allah's injunction to do good and serve the poor and needy. But it also brought this injunction home, says Waris Malik, who chaired the team that put on the soup day. "If we can do this for an overseas project, why can't we do it for our own neighborhood " he remembers thinking. "Toronto's multiculturalism is so rare and enriching, I wanted to enrich that, not just be part of it," he says.

David Suzuki, Canada's green folk hero, gave members of the Islamic Foundation their opportunity, when they led and hosted a multi-faith dinner and public meeting at their mosque on the spirituality of environmentalism for 700 people in January. The mosque became "Allah's house, not our house, and everyone was welcome," says Azeez, a mainstay of inter-faith activities in the Malvern area.

The Suzuki event got rid of some of the anti-Muslim prejudices created by 9/11 media coverage, and created both good will and a cause for doing something at home, says Arshia Alam, a teacher at the Mosque school and another coordinator of the hot soup day. "I was on board right away," she says, having helped at food banks and soup kitchens during her student days at University of Toronto.

A person who denies God is also a person who doesn't see the need to feed the needy, it says in the *Quran*. Food is also the most obvious way to help all people in need, regardless of cultural or religious background.

The hot soup day didn't coincide only with Easter weekend. Earlier the same week, Statistics Canada released its report predicting that "visible minorities" will become the majority in major cities by 2017, the year Canada celebrates its 150th birthday.

Toronto's Community Social Planning Council also released its report on inclusive cities. The report calls on governments to become proactive in implementing policies that prevent the hardening of gender, ethno-racial and poverty divisions that have become more ominous after 15 years of government cutbacks.

Ironically, the report barely refers to food, a basic need that transcends gender, race and income, and a basic vehicle for promoting inclusion.

This omission may reflect a professional bias embedded among planning professionals, a reflection perhaps of a time when hunger and famine ceased to be defining social policy issues in the English-speaking world. This may explain why pre-professionalized groups, such as churches, have been at the forefront of naming hunger as an urgent policy issue. And it may be why Muslim mosques, serving members who, despite educational levels that far surpass the Canadian average, endure an unemployment rate that's double the average, understand the call to make hunger a priority issue, as well as a vehicle for creating community.

Mosque leaders plan to repeat the soup day that's been piloted, and to explore other initiatives that promote both food security and social engagement.

43

section two: Sustainable Food Systems

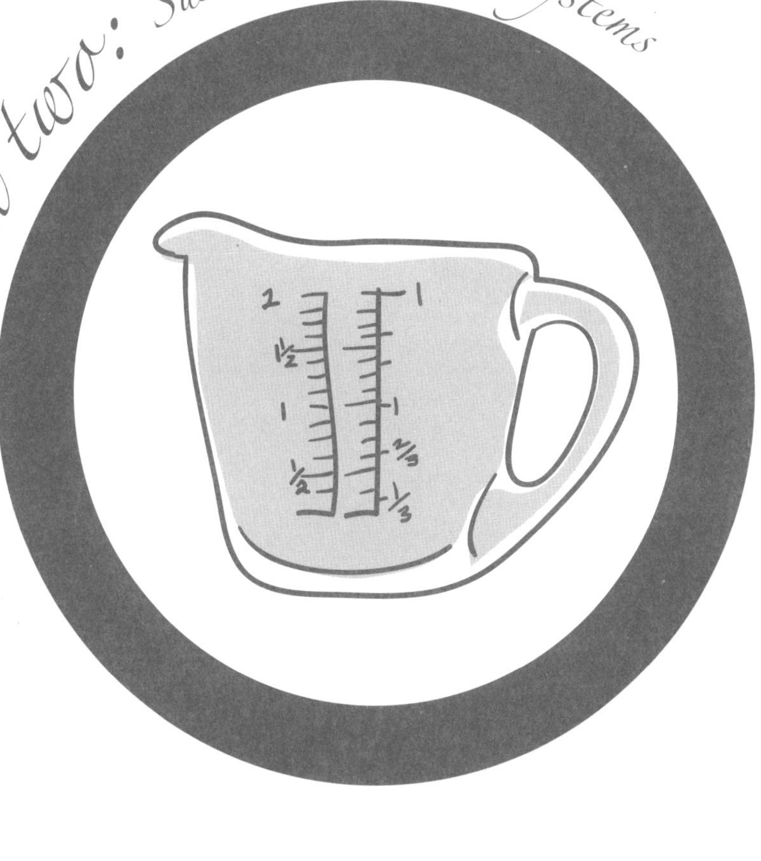

Wiens Shared Farm

Farming on a Friendly Scale
by Will Braun

At the Wiens Shared Farm, just south of Winnipeg, the notion of expansion is treated with suspicion. There are no plans to expand beyond the current 12 acres, no dreams of increased mechanization, no grand marketing schemes. For the seven Wiens Farm workers—who operate as a collective—scale is vital, and a small, friendly scale operation is central to their concept of farming and food.

The Wiens Shared Farm, which started in 1992, functions on the Community Shared Agriculture model. About 100 shares are sold to Winnipeg residents who make a single payment in spring and receive weekly deliveries of in-season vegetables throughout the harvest season. Selling the full number of shares is never a problem. Produce is also sold at two farmer's markets. The Wiens Farm produces a full range of vegetables with the exception of potatoes, which are ill-suited to the riverside soil.

The focus of the farm is on maximizing local integration. Virtually all food grown on the farm is eaten with 35 kilometres of the field. The farmers take satisfaction in providing trustworthy food directly from grower to eater. They believe that she who plants, weeds and harvests the food should also be the person who delivers the food directly to the eater. It's food with relationship. A small-scale operation makes this possible.

At the Wiens Shared Farm, "organic" is only one element of producing trustworthy food. In addition to organic fertilizer and pest control, minimized mechanization (and hence, reduced use of fossil-fuel burning equipment), minimized transportation and provision of non-processed foods (processing is energy intensive) are part of truly organic food. Again, a larger scale operation would increase pressure to mechanize and increase transportation inputs.

One of the most valued aspects of local integration at the Wiens Farm is partnership with the Good Food Club, an inner-city initiative that promotes healthy living and builds community through good food. Club members spend a few days a week working on the farm in exchange for fresh vegetables. The Good Food Club also sells Wiens vegetables at highly affordable rates at an inner-city community centre on Saturdays. The three-year-old partnership between the farm and the club provides a mutually enriching rural-urban connection.

One ingredient of the sustained viability of the farm is the collective manner in which its workers function. The seven collective members share risks, responsibilities, earnings and decision making. The collective rents the farm from Dan and Wilma Wiens, who started the farm and continue to participate in the collective.

The collective model means the pressures of an intensive growing season do not fall to just one person or family. Also, the diversity of ideas and skills is considered as valuable as crop/bio-diversity in promoting sustainability. And working together is simply more fun than working alone. Farming must be viable not only economically but also in terms of farmer morale and spiritual well-being. A collective model in which multiple people have a strong sense of ownership is vital in this regard.

The modest scale of the operation is conducive to collective functioning.

The Wiens farmers are intentional about de-corporatizing a food chain that has become concentrated around a handful of agri-food giants whose focus and mandate are, profit not good food. Each carrot grown truly organically and locally displaces a corporately grown carrot. Ultimately, there is no way to overcome corporate mismanagement of the food chain unless people grow good, locally integrated food. This, by nature, must be done on a scale that is antithetical to the corporate überscale. The Wiens Farm workers take satisfaction in knowing that by providing their vegetables, they offer people the chance to exit the corporate food system.

The Wiens Shared Farm experience demonstrates that demand for trustworthy vegetables in the Winnipeg area is considerably greater than current supply. The answer to this welcome challenge is not increased size of existing farms but an increase in the number of small, friendly scale farms.

A Fresh New Guide

by Sharon Taylor

Somewhere between the nearest drive-thru and the ever-proliferating big box stores, we've lost our connection to the land and to our local producers. Our very relationship with food has changed in our time-intensive, lo-carb world. We rarely question where our food comes from and how it's grown or raised, perhaps because it's a virtually impossible question to answer.

To the large corporations, under our existing economic policy, food is nothing more than a commodity. Most of it is grown thousands of kilometres away on industrial farms, not for taste or nutrition, but for aesthetic perfection and ease of transport. We all know how ridiculous it is that our strawberries come from California, even in season, and we complain bitterly that they taste like cardboard. Mad Cow tramples our dinner-table conversation, lowing fearfully about the financial and health ramifications of the disease. New studies are published, daily it seems, about the effects of pesticides and Genetically Modified Organisms (GMOs) on our ecosystems and on our bodies. Industrial agriculture isn't sustainable, and it doesn't satisfy the requirements of food security.

More and more people are taking a stand, searching for fresher, tastier, quality food from local sources and striving to renew their connection with the earth.

At the heart of Food Security in Manitoba beats a progressive and inspiring organic movement. The Organic Food Council of Manitoba (OFCM), a local chapter of Canadian Organic Growers (COG), reports that there are at least 300 certified organic producers in Manitoba and over 100 farms in transition. Throughout the province, there are more than 120 businesses selling organic food or providing services to organic farmers and gardeners. Rousing numbers!

From fresh veggies to organic beef, bison, poultry and pork, to orchards, herbs and grains; we even have an organic winery! Here in Manitoba, we eat well. Yet, the industry is still somewhat fragmented, which makes it vulnerable to the whims of the large corporations. We need to continue to encourage our local farmers and business owners by purchasing more of our food locally, and OFCM has just published the perfect resource to help us do it.

Down to Earth – Guide to Organics in Manitoba is OFCM's freshly updated directory of organic farms and businesses in Manitoba (and a few in Saskatchewan and northwestern Ontario). It's juicy with articles, explanations and news stories about the local organic scene; ripe with titbits that will inspire our imaginations. But this directory is not just a listing, not simply a source of information about food security and reasons to go organic. *Down to Earth* is much more than the sum of its parts.

We, as consumers, hold the power of change in our hands, and this directory compels us to make the changes we wish to see in the world. In simply taking the first step and purchasing *Down to Earth*, we are supporting OFCM's initiatives in Manitoba.

We're helping to educate young farmers and to revive agriculture in the province. Some of us still remember the days (or remember the stories of the days) when small, diverse farms and thriving rural communities quilted the prairies, when neighbours came together to raise barns and bring in the harvest. More and more people are leaving the cities and setting up homesteads on small acreages, chasing after simplicity. By encouraging and supporting those brave hardy souls, we play an integral role in restoring the beautiful prairie tapestry.

Down to Earth engages us to take action, to become a part of a growing movement, to educate ourselves and our children about sustainability and the importance of agricultural diversity. Every farmer who is listed in the directory has written a few words about their operation. They are the people who grow the food that sustains us. We can choose to purchase directly from them, either from the farm gate or at farmers markets. Or, we can explore the corner grocery stores in our own neighbourhoods or in neighbouring communities. We can choose to eat seasonally, locally or low on the food chain. If we are compelled to, we can go a step further. We can form or join food buying clubs or we can create municipal food policies. With our dollars, we influence our corporate world. When we choose to purchase local organic products, we speak out, both as individuals and in solidarity with each other. All people, at all times, have the right to sufficient, safe and nutritious food. All farmers around the world have the right to save their seeds and make a fair wage. Here in Manitoba, we are blessed with wealth and the freedom to both demand and inspire these rights, for ourselves and for all people who share the earth.

In supporting OFCM and the organic producers in Manitoba, we are supporting sustainabililty, stewardship of the land and the ethical treatment of animals. On a local level, we will revitalize our economy, improve our health and the health of our soil and wildlife and influence positive change in our communities.

On a global level, by connecting with farmers in Manitoba, we will strengthen our connection with producers the world over, who labour to bring us food staples like rice, bananas and coffee. By supporting organics here at home, our money will no longer subsidize destructive, polluting, exploitative farming practices in developing countries.

Down to Earth – Guide to Organics in Manitoba answers the question, "Where does our food come from?" and it gives us the means to ask, "How was it grown or raised?" It exists because we want this kind of information, right now. Whether we are experiencing the beginning of a Green Revolution, or simply a shift in perspective, it is an evocative time of change and reform. In using *Down to Earth*, we can explore our relationship with food and our interconnectedness with the earth. In nourishing our bodies, we nourish our spirits, and with our spirits nourished, there's no telling what we can achieve.

Down to Earth – Guide to Organics in Manitoba is available at all urban and rural (Manitoba-based) stores that sell local, quality food. It sells for $6.95, with the proceeds going to the education and promotion work of the OFCM. If you want to purchase a number of copies for an event or a small group, contact Sharon Taylor at (204) 779-8546 or staylox@hotmail.com. Bulk copies (ten or more) sell for six dollars each, plus shipping.

The BC Food Systems Network

by Cathleen Kneen

The BC Food Systems Network was initiated in 1999 as part of a project to increase public understanding of food policy. Its first act was to coordinate presentations to the provincial government's Standing Committee on Agriculture, Food and Fisheries, which held hearings on "agri-food policy" in the fall of 1999. Thanks to the collaboration of the members of the network, the committee was told at every stop along their way that food security requires a sustainable food system and is an essential goal of agri-food policy.

Since that time, the network has grown in numbers and in scope, so that its members now cover the entire province and represent an enormous diversity of interests related to food production, processing, distribution, consumption and quality. Over the years, the network has benefited from significant First Nations leadership, in particular in making the links between food and medicine and, more recently, food and land, from their traditional perspectives.

Three elements facilitate the Network: an electronic list-serv (and Web site), which keep members up-to-date on events and analysis relating to sustainable food systems and food security; an annual gathering in Sorrento, which provides an opportunity for learning, sharing information, and developing stronger relationships in the context of both formal and informal sessions – and exceptionally good food; and a coordinator who works part-time and mostly as a volunteer to maintain communications and help carry the vision forward.

The vision of the Network is contained in its definition of food security and its statement of purpose/process:

1. By food security we mean a sustainable food system in which:

- everyone is able to acquire, in a dignified manner, adequate quantity and quality of personally acceptable food.

- people are able to earn a living wage by growing, producing, processing, handling, retailing and serving food;

- the quality of land, air and water are maintained and enhanced for future generations; and

- food is recognized as the basis of health and celebrated as central to community and cultural integrity.

2. We recognize that food is essential to life and is therefore a human right. It is also a gift from the Creator so that both the food and its sources must be honoured.

3. We encourage initiatives to reclaim local ownership of community food systems and develop food self-reliance by sharing information, skills and resources.

4. We develop and advocate policies to redesign all systems contributing to hunger and unsustainable food systems, including but not limited to health, welfare, education, economic, trade, institutional, food production, processing, transport and food retail systems.

5. We work to ensure that the voices of grassroots organizations and marginalized groups are heard in the process of policy formation at all levels.

6. We link provincially, nationally and internationally with organizations and networks committed to the same goals.

The network makes decisions by consensus and considerable consultation (usually by email) ensures that policies adopted between the annual meetings reflect the perspectives of the whole organization.

The first task of the Network was to demystify the idea of "policy" and make the process of policy formation accessible to everyone, including people with personal experience of food insecurity. We did this by using the concept of a "personal food policy," which enables people to see that policy is simply the framework within which decisions are made, and that each of us has policies that guide our personal decisions. The challenge, then, in a democratic society, is to ensure that public policies reflect the priorities of the citizens, such as healthy food, a clean environment, local sources of food and access to food-related skills.

The first public policies addressed by the network were in the area of health. Food security is an essential element of public health, whether from the perspective of First Nations spirituality (which holds that food and medicine are closely linked and are often two ways of looking at the same thing) or from the perspective of chronic disease prevention. The organization has looked to its members who are directly involved in the health system as nutritionists, physicians, health officers and other public health workers to carry this analysis into policy making.

The formation of the Public Health Alliance on Food Security was an important move in this direction.

A second major focus has been skills building. Many of the members of the Network are involved in community-based projects and programs that increase skills in growing, choosing or processing food, and the annual Gathering provides an opportunity for leaders in these programs to share ideas and experiences and for others to gain basic skills through workshops such as: composting, cooking with kids, making bread, seed saving, traditional food gathering and processing, dehydrating food – as well as organizational skills such as fundraising, deconstructing propaganda and working with the media.

In the past year, with the growing acceptance of the importance of food security by many influential people in the field of public health, the network has begun to focus on food system sustainability – an essential aspect of food security. This involves increased efforts to ensure that people involved in commercial food production, processing, and distribution are encouraged to participate in all roundtables and forums. It has also led the network into alliances for public education and advocacy on issues that have been raised by our farmer members, in particular the integrity of the seed supply and the viability of local abattoirs in BC. In these efforts we are partnering with organizations such as the Island Farmers Alliance, the Certified Organic Associations of BC, the National Farmers Union and the Beyond Factory Farming Coalition.

At the same time, we continue to encourage the development of local and regional food-security policy organizations in BC and to work with alliances concerned with food security and food policy, both within BC and nationally. We look forward to the consolidation of a national food-security policy organization within the next year.

Winnipeg's Community Gardens

by Karen Lind and Stéphane McLachlan

How do drinking and driving, illegal drug use and littering make a great food-security initiative? Directly, they don't. Rather, the successful public-awareness and education campaign strategies that were mounted regarding those issues could serve as models for a food-security strategy. Public-awareness and education campaigns are effective tools for influencing societal values and creating change.

Public awareness around the issue of food security has a head start because everyone has an active, daily relationship with food. The rationale for most food-security awareness campaigns is based on the fact that many people have trouble securing enough good-quality food to meet their needs. One of the inherent weaknesses of many food-security campaigns, however, is that they foster feelings of despair or hopelessness as people come to understand the complexities of the issue.

A fundamental ingredient for preventing negative or paralyzing public sentiment is the need to maintain optimism by sharing in the successes, as embodied by publications such as the one you hold in your hand. Celebrating successful food-security initiatives helps keep the ball rolling and can prevent us from becoming overwhelmed by the magnitude of the problem. Another initiative with the same "celebration" mandate currently being undertaken in Winnipeg focusses on the connections between community gardening and broader social, environmental and economic issues.

Increasing Winnipeg Community Garden Visibility

Community gardens are an increasingly popular method of addressing local food security by providing an environmentally sustainable, alternative food system capable of increasing accessibility to and the availability of fresh, often organically, produced food for both participants and non-participants. Winnipeg is home to over 30 community gardens operating through a variety of organizations, including horticultural societies, neighbourhood associations, church groups, daycares and schools. Like many other cities, Winnipeg's community gardens face a variety of challenges–especially land tenure and water accessibility–that threaten their continued existence and potential expansion, and require the attention of municipal governments. But in comparison with other Canadian urban centres, Winnipeg's community gardens generally are not recognized by governments and the public, which limits the potential of these unique green spaces.

Initially, my involvement with some of Winnipeg's community gardens was of an academic nature, with Stéphane McLachlan at the University of Manitoba. I chose to focus my Master's project on the role of food security in women's community gardening experience. I was motivated to validate community gardens beyond their hobby status, believing, if I could illustrate how they were contributing to women's personal and household food security, that the city would be more likely to support and promote the existing and future gardens. However, residents need to be aware of the benefits and challenges confronting community gardens if they are to influence government and policy makers.

With this realization, I started to see the importance of increasing public support rather than just producing a two-page policy recommendation based on my academic work. I no longer viewed this project in terms of the work I was going to do (such as convince government to support community gardens) and instead saw it in terms of celebrating the great work that others were doing.

I began to understand that creating a public-awareness and education campaign with the sole focus on policy change or governmental support was naïve, and gave too much influence to policy makers. As I became aware of the diversity of benefits that participants were attributing to the gardens, some only indirectly related to the production of food or food security, I realized the potential risk of undermining these testimonies by focussing on one or two arguments I had assumed contributed to the need for community garden support. I required a new lens through which to look at this project. Rather than putting all my eggs in one policy basket, I realized that if policy change did not result from this campaign, it was better to create an opportunity for citizens to celebrate in and share their inspiring achievements.

The one challenge to any public-awareness and education campaign is making it truly public. Very often awareness and education campaigns inadvertently target specific populations–frequently those already involved or aware of the issue–and often fail to include those who are targeted. This "preaching to the converted" is difficult to overcome and the main problem that needed to be addressed while brainstorming around creating a community garden public-awareness and education tool. The specific format we required was one that could represent as many voices and experiences as possible so as to create a widely applicable and effective tool for citizens, practitioners and politicians. It didn't take long to realize that a video-based awareness tool was appropriate, but more importantly that it should also be a collaborative approach directly involving community members in the development and creation process.

Although still in the production phase, the themes that have been and are going to be explored throughout this video have come directly from community gardeners, members and workers. Food security was definitely one of the main themes identified, but it is explored and reflected in many different ways. For some, the garden has increased their accessibility to what they identify as quality, very often organic, food (in contrast with "the hard rubber balls you buy in the store"), while for others the garden plays a substantial economic role. Most significant is the great number of gardeners, these representing a full spectrum of socio-economic backgrounds, who appreciated the importance of knowing exactly where their food comes from and of actively playing a role in the production process, and that this is how community gardens contribute to their food security.

This video is also exploring additional themes affecting both the gardeners and larger community, including social and ecological benefits, health and well-being contributions, community development/mobilization support, inter-generational connections, experiential knowledge exchange and valuation, as well as the challenges to community gardening. Factoring in these associated topics illustrates how initiatives addressing food security simultaneously address other issues and, although they may not solve our food security problem, they still need to be appreciated for their other contributions. Gardeners also thought it important to have a section or chapter (which DVDs now allow for) specifically dedicated to garden and gardening techniques, including tips on decreasing vandalism, composting garden waste, saving seeds, companion planting, accessible garden design, organic pest management and water conservation, to name just a few.

In keeping with the celebration theme, a series of free, public, outdoor video premiere evenings are scheduled for the end of August. Along with viewing the video in the garden, a community feast and other forms of entertainment will be included.

This particular video premierè enhances the community garden public-awareness campaign by providing a unique and festive experience. Free copies of the video will then be made available to schools, libraries, community groups, environmental associations, municipal councillors horticulture societies and, of course, the community gardens.

This initiative intends to increase both public and governmental support for Winnipeg's community gardens. The video allows gardeners to play a direct role in educating all stakeholders about community gardening and why it deserves more recognition. And it is also meant to pay tribute to such encouraging initiatives and take time to celebrate some of the ways food security is being addressed within our city.

The Centre for Studies in Food Security

by Mustafa Koc

Established as a research centre out of the faculties of arts and community services at Ryerson University in 1994, the Centre for Studies in Food Security (CSFS) has been working towards the university's mission by facilitating dialogue, research, community action and professional practice, to increase food security by focussing on issues of health, income and the evolution of the food system, including attention to ecological sustainability and socio-cultural diversity.

The centre has a special focus on the unique organization and problems of urban and metropolitan food systems and the way in which these systems are linked to the rural community and agricultural sector. The activities of the centre reflect its commitment to the integration of research, education and practice initiatives, as well as a local and global orientation to food security issues. The centre aims:

- to facilitate dialogue for research, community action, business developments and professional practice in food security

- to contribute to the knowledge base on food security through development of a research and consulting capacity that draws on the strengths of faculty and students, and on Ryerson's commitment to applied research and professional education.

- to generate research and innovative practices responsive to societal need, in partnership with community groups, small businesses, producers' organizations, health professionals, universities, government agencies and others

- to share information and resources across all sectors, utilizing electronic media, publications, conferences, public forums, network meetings and other means of participatory development communication

Food Security Certificate

The centre, in partnership with the School of Nutrition and the Division of Continuing Education at Ryerson University, offers a six-course distance education certificate. The Certificate in Food Security supports community agencies and practitioners, not only through the process of education and providing credentials, but also as the educational experience allows for research projects and "real world" initiatives for problem solving. The certificate provides applied and professional training to help students:

- articulate food security and its relationship to food system, food policy and health promotion concepts

- assess and monitor individuals, households, communities or nations for food security

- identify the forces contributing to food security and insecurity at an individual, household, community or national level

- identify best practices for food security from within Canada and other nations

- design effective and integrated programs, services or policies at the individual, household, community or national level to contribute to food security

- evaluate the effectiveness of food security programs and policy

The certificate requires completion of three core courses and three elective among several offered through Ryerson University. Courses in Portuguese will also be available in the near future. The CSFS aims to offer courses in other languages in the coming years in collaboration with its institutional partners.

CIDA-UPCD Tier II Project: Building Capacity in Food Security in Brazil

The training and dissemination capacity of the centre was central to the recent CIDA-UPCD funding of the project to provide community-based education and training models in Brazil and Angola. The project, with an overall budget of $1.6 million, is undertaken in collaboration with the Reference Centre for Food and Nutrition Security at the Rural Federal University of Rio de Janeiro, Brazil. The initiative will provide community-based education and training models that respond to the development challenge of increasing food security for the most vulnerable populations in developing countries, and in particular in Brazil and Angola. It will focus on the formation of social actors in food and nutrition security in the poorest region of Brazil and will involve the piloting of new programs in food security with civil society organizations and local governments in three northeastern regions of Brazil. A number of complementary research projects are also planned.

In partnership with a number of civil society, government and academic organizations, the Centre is in the process of developing a research program for improving food security by strengthening the structural capacity of civil society organizations (CSOs) to work collaboratively with governments. This project aims to improve methodologies for food security analysis by developing a common framework for national and community food security indicators and tools for evaluating outcomes,

to generate new knowledge to enhance CSO capacity in food security research and policy development and to strengthen regional and national CSO efforts in networking and collaboration.

Creating a Platform for Dialogue

In addition to research and education, the CSFS believes that academic institutions have an important role to play in addressing societal issues through the creation of public forums and networks to achieve closer cooperation and effective communication among public sector and civil society organizations. In support of the many actors in food security (locally, nationally and globally), the centre has organized seminars, conferences and electronic list-serves. In the 1990s the centre organized a Toronto–based local network (Toronto Food Research Network) and manages the national list-serve called Food-Democracy in an attempt to link with a broader network of academics, practitioners, policy makers and concerned citizens in Canada.

The CSFS has hosted two international conferences, the International Conference on Sustainable Urban Food Systems (1997) and Crossing Borders: Food & Agriculture in the Americas (1999), and was involved in organizing workshops on food security in Rio de Janeiro (2000) and at the World Social Forum in Porto Alegre, Brasil (2001). In 2001, the CSFS also hosted a national conference, Working Together: Civil Society Working for Food Security in Canada, at Ryerson (2001), which brought together members of Canadian civil society organizations working for food security. Members of the centre have been active in initiatives to shape local and national food policy and in other regional and national food-security advocacy efforts.

The Seasoned Spoon

*Cultivating a Student run
Food Security Initiative*
by Karen Sutherland,
Jessi Dobyns, and Karine Rogers

The Seasoned Spoon Café is a student-run non-profit cooperative on the campus of Trent University that serves locally grown and organic foods, does research into alternative food and agricultural systems, and is always trying out new recipes for community food security.

Starting with Stone Soup–A pot of water, a stone, and not much more

Four years ago, a group of Trent University students joined together to form the Food Issues Group (FIG). At our first meeting, it became evident that all of us wanted an alternative to the food offered by Aramark, the corporate food service provider on campus. We wanted a real alternative that would operate under a particular set of guidelines, The food sourced would be locally grown, as much as possible, and ideally from organic, fair trade suppliers when not. We wanted to be as energy efficient as possible and to serve all food on non-disposables – the business would recycle and compost. It would be run as a non-profit cooperative, be accessible and affordable, and, perhaps most importantly in negotiating permission from Aramark to sell food, the café we envisaged would conduct research into alternative food-systems provisioning for the local community through applied research for credit projects.

We began as the "Stone Soup" project. Aramark has an exclusivity agreement with Trent University that effectively grants them a monopoly over all food served on campus. Wanting to serve soup on a somewhat regular basis, FIG applied for an exemption granting us permission to sell soup, by donation, in the student hall. People rarely asked for formal exemptions from the monopoly, but the university administration and Aramark had no good grounds to refuse us and after a couple of months of stalling we were given permission to serve soup a couple of times.

As a student group of OPIRG (Ontario Public Interest Research Group), FIG had an annual budget of $100.00–which is not really enough to set up a soup stand. We went to local farmers asking for food donations with the understanding that we would "donate" back when/if we raised the funds. We gathered together what equipment we collectively had and bought second-hand dishes and an electric hotplate. We asked the local health inspector to certify a member's home kitchen and then we started cooking.

Every time we set the Stone Soup table up, an industrial-sized pot of soup sold out in under an hour. People gathered in the hall, eating and chatting and telling us how very, very grateful they were for this food. While we were all volunteering our labour at this point, donations always more than covered our costs, making us able to pay farmers a fair price for the food we bought. Interest in this alternative was underlined by the fact that groups started asking us to cater events. We started making two pots of soup, trying to keep up with the demand, but to no avail–the soup sold out just as fast as the word spread. We quickly surpassed our capacity and started thinking more seriously about starting a café.

Having met with the Director of Student Affairs to obtain the first exemption, we began attempting to negotiate a larger exemption to open on a more regular basis. While we'd gotten our foot in the door, Aramark still had the right to take away our exemption at any point, or prevent us from expanding our operations. With growing support from the student body, faculty and staff, we continued Stone Soup the next academic year and got permission to open two days a week on campus, under the condition that we serve soup and only soup. We put together a founding board, wrote bylaws and developed the organizational structure, while also collecting more donations of supplies and money and trying to get a student pub space up to health codes for commercial cooking. In February of 2003 the Seasoned Spoon officially opened its doors, employing six staff and many more volunteers, and serving soup two days a week for two hours. We then ran a successful levy campaign in the student association's referendum, resulting in an annual two-dollar levy per full-time student.

In negotiating the exemption from Aramark's monopoly, the Spoon was able to demonstrate that Aramark's failure to allow us permission to operate would limit the type of academic research available at Trent, which is a strong argument to wage at an academic institution. The Spoon is now open four days a week, seven hours a day, and has managed to obtain a signed contract with the university and Aramark, allowing us to serve whatever food we choose, as long as we are not replicating Aramark's services. We employ a dozen kitchen and counter staff, an education and outreach position and a 30-hour a week coordinator.

Edible Treats and Educational Treatises

Academic research has been one of the most essential ingredients of the Spoon's success. The Spoon is not just a food service provider; it is also an experiential learning cooperative. Giving students the opportunity to do research for credit at the Spoon has greatly contributed to the Spoon's infrastructure and

at the same time has added legitimacy to the Spoon's right to exist as part of the university community. The breadth of the Spoon's mission statement means that students have the opportunity to do research in a wide variety of disciplines. So far, the Spoon has overseen seven student research projects in Administrative Studies to Environmental Science to International Development Studies. In some ways the Spoon acts as a coop program, where students are able to apply their academic experiences to a working organization, such as writing a business plan or developing the accounting structure for a non-profit business. These types of projects benefit the Spoon in terms of developing infrastructure while giving students the chance to learn in a hands-on, experiential way.

The Spoon is also committed to critical academic inquiry to help shape the organization within the context of alternative food and agricultural systems. This allows for self-reflection on how the Spoon is realizing its role as part of an alternative food system and gives students the chance to engage the academic side of food and agriculture. For example, two students are currently working on developing a sourcing policy for the Spoon that reflects the Spoon's commitments to local and organic production systems. This project builds on research done last year by students about the principles that inform the Spoon's sourcing, such as localism, organic agriculture, fair trade and foodshed systems.

The Spoon is also fortunate to be at a university with a Community-Based Education Centre that provides support to students to do research for credit with community organizations such as ours, as well as ample faculty support for doing research as part of existing courses, independent studies and reading courses. In addition, Trent has a new interdisciplinary Special Emphasis in Food and Agriculture, strengthening the link between the academic environment at Trent and the Spoon.

Access and Food Security

Operating on a university campus has provided unique infrastructural and other critical supports, including low overhead costs (no rent), partial wage subsidization from the Ontario government and roughly $9000 in guaranteed annual funding through a student levy, which have in effect allowed us to further realize our goals regarding food security. It allows us to keep food prices down while still paying full price to local food producers, in hopes of furthering an agenda for fair agricultural prices and community economic development. The Spoon does source wholesale goods from larger suppliers such as a local bakery, Sticklings and Ontario Natural Foods Co-op, but attempts to give priority to what is available directly from local farmers.

The down-side of operating on the university's main campus north of Peterborough is that our connection to the community rests largely with our relationship to suppliers, limiting potential relationships to both members of the wider Peterborough community and other food security initiatives in the city's centre.

Included in the Spoon's mission statement is a commitment to providing affordable food. The organization works towards this goal in several ways. All the food provided by the Stone Soup project that predated the Spoon was given out by donation, with a suggested price to recoup costs. In an attempt to honour this tradition, all bread at the Spoon is still sold by donation. And while the Spoon's prices are relatively low compared to similar endeavours ($2.50 for a hearty bowl of soup), the prices are still inevitably a barrier for some people. Membership prices are sliding scale, and all volunteers receive free food as remuneration, but there has yet to be serious consideration about creating more accessible pricing schemes, such as serving all food by sliding scale or donation. These are both attractive options to consider, particularly given the wide range of members' incomes, from tenured professors to university staff to indebted students.

Sometimes while eating lunch in the Spoon, we'll look around and marvel that it has actually made it this far, that we were able to break a solid corporate monopoly and have the opportunity to even try to encourage an alternative food system. It would not have happened without countless volunteer hours, a student levy and widespread support. It would not have happened without student research projects, which contributed not only academically, but also to the legitimacy of the organization. By developing the Spoon as an experiential learning centre, we gained leverage as part of the research community at the university, while also contributing to the growing interest in food and agricultural issues. And this learning is not limited to formal research projects: the Spoon creates a space that is ripe for discussion between students, staff and faculty about the larger issues in food security that inform this initiative, all over a tasty bowl of soup.

A more detailed recount of the Spoon's history is available at: www.trentu.ca/opirg/seasonedspoon.

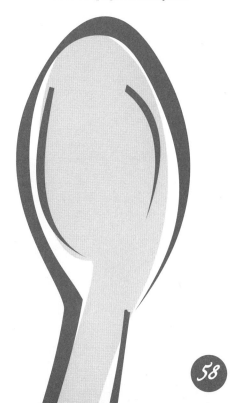

Choosing a Different Path

by David M. Neufeld

Early in 2002, a group of farmers from the Boissevain/Minto area (southwest Manitoba) started asking each other if there was more we could do to address depopulation and food insecurity in our community. And though we were a diverse lot–large, medium and smaller scale workers of the land–we agreed on two questions to guide us. One, how do we make farming more profitable and more attractive to our young people and to other new farmers? And two, what relationships/alliances do we need to nurture in order to get the support we need? We recognized immediately that to get more people interested in farming, we would need to slow and stop the trend toward every other farm becoming larger by swallowing up neighbouring lands. We decided to cast our eyes over our community to see if there were still smaller scale successful farms around and to give them a spotlight. We raised some local and provincial funds. It took us two years, but we managed to publish a book in which 20 local smaller scale, farm families were able to tell their stories and offer some teachings. We feel this is a significant contribution to the food security discussion.

We are in danger of losing sight of those farmers (potential teachers)who are maintaining the diverse skills needed to grow food and make a living off a small holding. Following is the introduction to our book entitled *Successful Small Farms in Southwest Manitoba*. (You can call 1-800-497-2393 for copies.)

Our aim is to attract more people to live and work on the land in our community. We want to highlight ways for people to make a living off less rather than more land. Please join us as we:

a. explore the viability of smaller scale farms as a choice for new, immigrant and down sizing farmers

b. offer some council for the process of designing a smaller scale farm and

c. suggest some contextual concerns that need to be answered or researched more deeply.

Please first, though, consider our collective dilemma. We, as a prairie society, want to continue growing and raising quality food for ourselves and for export, but we're steadily making it more difficult for our children to become farmers. Consequently, our rural population is shrinking and the goods and services we offer each other are becoming fewer. This state of affairs is not entirely of our own making, but it's up to us to turn the situation around. Southwest Manitoba is a wonderful place to live and I believe we dearly want our children to stay (or to go away for a time and return) to raise families and contribute to a vibrant, productive and creative rural society.

It has always been the task of agrarian societies to prepare the next generation of farmers – often against tough odds. Agrarian societies all over the world are (and all through the ages have been) vulnerable to being manipulated and undervalued by those who wield power. There have been countless peasant revolts and revolutions as workers of the land have resorted to violence to protect their way of life and to insist on fair returns for their labour.

It seems we're choosing a different way of protest. We're telling our children not to farm. Contrary to our deepest desires, we're sending them to the cities and small towns to do anything but grow food for a living.

The reasons behind this shift are numerous and complex. In a nutshell, most farm families want to have less debt, more income and more leisure time to be with family. Most of us feel the only way we can succeed is by farming more land and buying larger equipment. The price of land remains high due to the resultant competition for land. The costs of equipment and inputs are steadily rising and the prices we're getting for the crops we grow are essentially staying flat. This means we have more debt, less income and less leisure time, when all is tallied up. Why would we encourage our children to do this? There are options that appear to be more promising.

We increasingly hear each other commenting on our loss of nearby neighbours. Forty years ago, every half section of arable land had a homestead and a family with at least three children. In our municipality we've lost half our population in the last four decades. With the loss of population, our smaller towns are losing businesses, schools, churches, hospitals and ice rinks. We're not only losing people and institutions from the land and small towns, though. We're losing knowledge of the land and what it requires to sustain living communities (human and otherwise). We're losing hope for the future and, consequently, we're losing belief in our own worth and resourcefulness. And we're losing the will to turn the situation around. With this loss of will, we risk losing our place as keepers of fundamental human values: reverence for divine and cosmic influences, honest work with our hands, satisfaction in reaping the best food this good earth can provide and a unique appreciation for how our independence is coupled with community interdependence. If our children are to grow food, we want them to do it with passion and a strong sense of ownership – not as employees of distantly managed firms.

The up-side is that we're gaining farmers from more congested and regulated countries – like England, Holland and Germany. These immigrants see our big spaces and relatively low land prices as being their ticket to a more progressive, hassle-free life. We appreciate the enthusiasm and diversity this adds to our mix. We fear, though, that our new neighbours will have only a few good years before their imported equity runs thin and they abandon their vision within the first generation. We want more people on the land but we also want their choices to be well informed and their efforts to contribute to a sustainable community. Much as retiring farmers look toward imported money to ensure they can rest in comfort, the outside buyers they turn towards do keep our land prices out of reach for the local youth who want to farm. There's plenty of room for immigration. But we should not let it distract us from the bigger questions: How do we make sure the profits from farming stay close to home so that we can confidently encourage our own youth to farm? How do we discourage the upward spiral of land prices so our youth can afford to buy in? How do we (re)establish the farming of this land as a cooperative effort? Is it all about money?

Canadian farmers today are generating seven times the gross income they generated in 1970. But our net income has stayed the same. Even if we're uncertain about these numbers, we know how diligently our neighbours and we have responded to the push for higher production. Those who are willing to benefit extravagantly from the work and vulnerability of farmers, though, always skim off the profits from this higher production. History has shown that nobody – governments, churches, universities or benefit concerts—will turn this situation around unless rural communities give the lead. We've heard it said that we only have three sources of power these days: governments, corporations and civil society. Nothing much, history tells us, will change unless civil society convinces governments to act on their behalf.

Homemakers and retail food outlets are doing their bit by asserting their preference for local, fresh food of the highest quality. There are growing niches opening for smaller, market-savvy farmers. The process, though, of providing vision and leadership to agriculture policy on every level remains a constant challenge.

With our book *Successful Small Farms in Southwest Manitoba* we're adding a rare voice to that rising leadership – a collection of small farmers from one region. They don't profess to have all the answers to our dilemma. In fact, just about every one of them laughed when we suggested they might have something to show the world. You'll be hard-pressed to find fancy equipment on these yards and you may not be too impressed at first glance by their annual incomes, but you may be impressed with their values, their financial ratios and stability. They're not your out-front-raising-a-raucous kind of leaders. Rather, they prefer to lead by example if we care to look their way. We invite you to read the stories and decide for yourself if these farmers are successful – in the contexts of their communities and in the context of what we want prairie agrarian society to be for our children, grandchildren and the world around.

Food Security Initiatives at Providence Farm

by Lisa Kell and Mark Timmermans

Our land is abundantly varied and so are the talents of the people in our community. Since we see the possibility of being open to the needs of different groups, we focus on those not easily accepted elsewhere. Trusting in Providence, we are creating a faith-centered community that sees the Renewal of Life in the cycle of people caring for the soil and the soil nurturing the people–Providence Farm's Mission Statement.

Providence Farm lies nestled in the Cowichan Valley, on the east coast of British Columbia's Vancouver Island. The Sisters of St. Ann own the 400-acre property and lease it to the Vancouver Island Providence Community Association (VIPCA), a registered non-profit society. The members of VIPCA carry on the Sisters' tradition of service to the community by assisting individuals living with mental or physical disabilities, a condition often met by barriers to employment.

A variety of therapeutic training and rehabilitative programs are available at Providence Farm, made possible through partnerships with several community agencies, such as the Vancouver Island Health Authority, Mental Health & Addictions, and Community Living Services. With 400 acres of farmland,

we can offer programs from within the fields of agriculture and horticulture to animal husbandry. We have hay fields, a barn, 7500 square feet of nursery and greenhouses, three acres of market gardens, a hen house, an apple orchard, 65 acres of active field crops, and a Craft Barn where we do cooking and canning. Numerous activities related to food security happen every day at the farm, including growing produce from seed; caring for organic crops; harvesting produce and collecting seeds for future crops; preparing and sharing in daily nutritious lunches together; preparing produce for market, storage and eating; composting; caring for livestock; gathering eggs for market; processing value-added items from the fruits and vegetables that are grown on-site; and basic cooking skills.

Two programs at the farm – Greenways and the St. Ann's Garden Club – particularly make use of these activities. Greenways is open to individuals in the community living with mental illness, developmental disability and brain injury. The program is tailored to meet the needs of participants and to build on their strengths. Horticultural therapy is at the heart of it, but participants can also become involved in small-engine repair, furniture building and retailing. Greenways helps clients develop job skills while at the same time building confidence, boosting physical fitnessand facilitating the development of social skills.

Currently serving from 24 to 28 adults, the St. Ann's Garden Club is open to seniors with mental health issues. Participants engage in activities of their choice, such as gardening, walking, cooking, carpentry, crafts and socializing. Additional activities at the Farm include:

• Walking and crafts, all done in a social setting.

• Get-togethers. For example, every Friday the Open Door Society, a group for individuals recovering from the acute phase of mental illness, gathers at the farm.

• Sharing of meals. There is a hot dish prepared everyday in the Greenways program, but on Fridays the whole farm comes together for this meal, which is made from produce grown on the farm. This provides an opportunity for participants to enjoy some of the fruits of their labour.

Providence Farm boasts community allotment gardens available to the public for $20 per year. We currently have 89 plots developed by individuals and groups, and there is a waiting list. This initiative has created the opportunity for members of the community to make connections and interact with one another and the program participants at the farm. Presently underway is the renovation of the Providence House, the original building on the farm. This will create a new commercial kitchen, one of whose functions will be the reintroduction to our community, through teaching opportunities and community kitchens, of healthy eating and home-cooking with whole foods.

Also in development is a workshop on nutrition to be piloted at Providence Farm. Working with a facilitator, participants will learn to i) evaluate their current eating habits, ii) identify the nutrition goals outlined in Canada's Food Guide, iii) increase their healthy food choices, and iv) identify the barriers they face in meeting their nutrition goals. Through this workshop, participants will receive user-friendly nutrition information that encourages them to make healthy choices, while being supported in building relationships in the community and making the most of community resources. The work at Providence Farm addresses a central food-security issue: that individuals and communities should conduct ecologically sound, sustainable food production practices. Part of achieving food security involves promoting locally grown food and the interest of communities in taking more active roles in food production and distribution.

The people who attend the programs at Providence Farm are being given a chance to be "experts" and so also to acquire a sense of ownership and accomplishment in their work and greater confidence in themselves. By producing healthy, organic foods and making them available to those who can and cannot 'buy organic', our clients contribute – and have the satisfaction of knowing they contribute – to the community in which they live. Providence Farm is a truly therapeutic community: for the people who attend its programs and for the people of the Cowichan Valley.

Yes, a sustainable, secure food supply is possible. Providence Farm is a living embodiment of the possibility made reality. Clients develop skills, a community comes together and an inclusive, successful organic farm is the result.

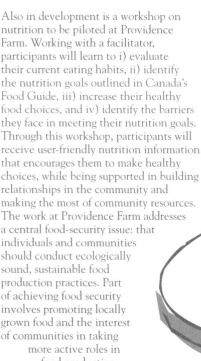
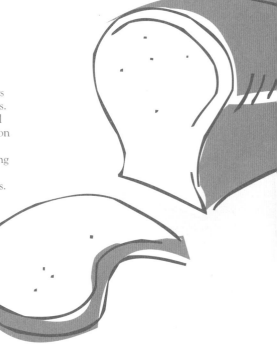

Harvesting Montreal's Rooftops

by Alex Hill and Jane Rabinowicz

Looking from a high-rise apartment window over downtown Montreal, you are immediately confronted by vast, untapped empty spaces. The monotonously grey expanse of residential and low-rise commercial rooftops appears as an infertile patchwork. But looking closer, you may see a few specs of green encroaching on the gravel and tar desert. Just as the Bedouin have adapted food production to the Sahara, so are urbanites adapting to the extremes of their environment. It is in this spirit that Santropol Roulant and Alternatives are implementing a mutual strategy for urban survival thorough rooftop gardening.

All over the world, rapidly growing cities are expanding into the most productive agricultural lands as economics, culture and history conspire to replace farms with suburbs. We are running headlong into a crisis where rising populations rely on shrinking farmlands. To avert or delay the crisis, food distribution is becoming more and more influenced by, and dependent on, international markets and the additional risks that these bring.

In these same cities, almost none of the food consumed is grown locally. People have become disconnected from the cycles that support their lives, having little knowledge of where their food is grown, how it is cultivated or how nutritious it is. Such dependence on outside sources to meet basic needs puts city-dwellers at greater risk of food insecurity. We are challenged to find ways to reintegrate food production into the cityscape, to reconnect people with the ecological and agricultural processes that sustain them.

Envisaging vegetable gardens on inner-city rooftops and opening these unused spaces to the community, Santropol Roulant and Alternatives set off to combine their experience and make this a reality. Santropol Roulant is a community organization that operates an innovative meals-on-wheels service, intergenerational activities and volunteer programs that aim to address the health and food-security needs of seniors and Montrealers living with a loss of autonomy. Alternatives, on the other hand, is an international development agency with a network of partners spanning more than 30 countries. Together they have devised a solution that could significantly alter the Canadian, and perhaps the global, cityscape.

Alternatives' international partners in mega-cities like Sao Paulo, Jakarta and Casablanca were looking for new ways to address urban poverty and dire inner-city environment conditions. High rates of population growth, income inequality, land degradation and soil erosion, as well as a host of institutional and economic factors that limit food security in the urban context, are causing endemic hunger in these cities. At the same time, partners in Mexico, Senegal and Cuba were experimenting with innovative hydroponics and organic agriculture techniques that reduce the cost and limitations of producing vegetables on degraded lands and in cities.

Thus, Alternatives began a program to share and demonstrate ideas that tackle food security and hunger issues around the world.

Starting in 2001, Alternatives (with the financial support of the International Development

Research Council) began to bring these ideas together and experiment with them in a garden on a Montreal garage roof.

The work focussed on adapting systems devised at the Institute of Simplified Hydroponics in Mexico to the Canadian context. From there, Alternatives began other action research projects in Morocco, Senegal and Cuba, in each case incorporating local concepts of organic and urban agriculture, and adapting the techniques tested in Montreal to other climates.

Santropol Roulant became interested in rooftop gardening when they first looked into setting up a garden on their own offices in 2000. Unfortunately, accessing their rooftop was not possible, so they sought another site while contributing ideas and volunteers to Alternatives' experimental garden. In the summer of 2004, Santropol Roulant and Alternatives together established a 500-square metre garden on the roof of a University of Quebec building located in the Plateau neighbourhood of Montreal. This volunteer-run rooftop demonstration garden now serves as a long-term learning ground while producing fresh food for the Santropol Roulant meals-on-wheels program.

Santropol Roulant's staff and volunteers see rooftop gardening as a key to strengthening food security in Montreal. Many volunteers live in the crowded city centre and have no access to a garden of their own. Santropol Roulant's collective rooftop garden offers them a place to experiment with urban agriculture, while encouraging participation in an enriching and enjoyable community activity. Through this work the gardeners themselves, who are mostly young people, are demonstrating a growing interest in issues regarding food security and sustainability.

The critical element of this work has been the combination of various ideas to create lightweight, simple-to-use and affordable gardens that can be built on flat rooftops in other small urban spaces or on degraded lands.

The rooftop gardens combine the principles of hydroponics, organic agriculture and permaculture to create a versatile set of garden designs.

"Hydroponics" refers to the growing of vegetables without the use of soil, wherein the nutrients are delivered directly to the roots by dissolving them in an irrigating solution. While hydroponics systems are usually complicated and expensive – requiring a variety of pumps and specialized materials – the rooftop gardens employ hydroponics in a way that requires no pumps and is constructed from materials that are easily found either at the recycling centre or the local hardware store.

The main advantage of this "simplified" form of hydroponics is that most of the weight (about 95%) is attributable to the nutrient solutions that feed and irrigate the plants. Thus, when the systems are drained of their water in the fall and turned upside-down for winter storage, they leave little additional weight on the rooftop. In Montreal, where inner-city roofs are flat and designed to hold over 20 pounds of snow per square foot, the rooftop gardens take advantage of the natural load-bearing capacity of the rooftops in the summer, but do not risk causing structural damage during the winter months when the gardens are stored empty. This is a significant step forward for rooftop gardening in cold climates, as it eliminates the need to invest in the expensive infrastructure retrofits that soil-based rooftop gardening requires.

The gardeners and researchers in Montreal, Cuba, Senegal and Morocco are now looking at ways to replace the chemical hydroponics nutrient solutions with compost-derived and organic nutrient sources. This will make the gardens even easier and cheaper to construct, making them a viable income-generation alternative for urban poor around the world.

Moreover, the sealed-container growers used in the Montreal rooftop garden do not lose water to infiltration and evaporation, which significantly reduces irrigation needs, providing yet another incentive for their use.

In Montreal the work is focussing on the research and adaptation of rooftop growing techniques.

With the support of Environment Canada, Health Canada, the City of Montreal and the Quebec Ministry of the Environment, Alternatives and Santropol Roulant are developing a how-to manual and a ready to go start-up kit to help individual home owners and renters start their own gardens. They are working with other community gardening and poverty-alleviation organizations to spread the idea of rooftop gardening through a wider network of demonstration sites and workshops. Over the coming three years, the ultimate goal is to integrate considerations for rooftop gardening into city building codes, and to establish a training and supply service through the Montreal Botanical gardens.

As these elements continue to fall into place, it will not be long before all high-rise apartment dwellers will be treated to a city covered in greenery. And, most important, Montrealers will all be able to enjoy the experience of eating freshly harvested summer vegetables that they grew by their own hand.

My First Time Buying Local

by Jessica Thornton

I never paid much attention to the food I bought. I tried to purchase food I knew I liked, that looked fresh, and I typically chose brands with which I grew up. While I never thought too much about where the fruits and vegetables came from, the meat I eat is mostly from my hometown butcher, who purchases from local farmers. My family has used this butcher for as long as I can remember. My mother always says that even though it costs a little more, it tastes so much better. She's also been on a first-name basis with the butcher since I was five, which definitely keeps her from going somewhere else. Now that I've moved away from home, my mother brings me large amounts of meat, which I freeze, every time she visits. However, if it were not for this, I would probably just buy whatever meat was at the grocery store.

I knew that buying/eating organic was better, but I am a student whose summer job money has run out, and buying the very cheapest fresh food is a necessity for me.

And then I read *Real Food for a Change*.

I came to understand the benefits of buying organic and/or local. Three days later, on my weekly grocery trip, I set out to Kensington Market on an organic/local produce mission.

As it was January, I soon realized that in terms of fruit, I was pretty much limited to Ontario apples or organic fruits from Mexico, California and Costa Rica. I chose apples, a fruit I've come to overlook lately.

For vegetables, I bought organic lettuce, celery and squash. The squash was local as well – bonus! I was delighted to find a five-pound bag of Ontario carrots for only $1.99. Usually I buy a bag of baby carrots for the same price and less than half the carrots. I also purchased a large bunch of Ontario radishes ($.99), a two-pound bag of Ontario parsnips ($.99), a bag of Ontario sprouts ($.49) and a large bag of Canadian tomatoes ($4.49). While "Canadian" isn't exactly local, it was either that, Costa Rican tomatoes, or doing without. As tomatoes take the leading role in my diet, I opted for the "Canadian" ones.

I stopped at the bakery for a loaf of whole wheat bread, prepared on-site. I left the market having spent roughly $14.50, only $.50 more than usual.

I'd also bought types of produce I don't usually buy. For the past few months, I've been finding that I go into a store with intentions of buying something different from the last time, but somehow still end up leaving with almost exactly the same food as the times before. This time I left the market with several foods I hadn't eaten in ages. Not only was I excited about the different things I could do with these foods (as well as different tastes), I also felt good about varying my consumption of fruits and vegetables, instead of relying on just a few old favourites.

Over the next few days, I had fun looking up recipes on the Internet and experimenting with new, exciting and delicious ways of preparing the fresh food.

The most delectable of these experiments was radishes baked in cinnamon and honey until they're soft: easily the tastiest radishes I'd ever had!

As for the apples – I don't remember the last time I had such a flavourful apple. I realized that the main reason I'd stopped eating apples was because the non-organic supermarket kinds were so tasteless. It had never occurred to me that there was any reason why those humungous apples tasted like nothing. I have patched up my relationship with apples and am now eating one daily.

It is true that buying local/organic is a little more time-consuming. I first had to look around to locate the local or organic food. I was lucky; a lot of the organic was together and had organic stickers. However, I had to look at every individual sign to decipher which food was local. A "local" sticker would have been very helpful. As well, some stores in the market do not tell where their food is from. After locating the local/organic food, I would compare what was there, decide how much I could afford to spend and finally make my purchase. In the past I would have walked into the store, grabbed what looked good and was affordable and have been out of there in half the time. However, once I got home and ate the local organic food, I realized it really was worth the extra shopping time! It tasted better, stayed fresh longer and I had a fantastic time experimenting with it.

I have to confess that I have not completely converted and I really cannot afford to buy organic food right now. Also, I still guiltily eat bananas. Having done a project in grade 12 on the treatment of banana plantation workers, I have not been able to eat one guilt-free since. Alas, they are cheap, nutritious and energizing, so, until I'm rich, they will be part of my diet.

Since I cannot always afford organic, I am left buying local, which I almost prefer to some extent anyway. I like the idea of supporting Ontario farmers. However, when buying local, I could not help but wonder how much pesticides were used on the food I was buying and how the workers were treated (I wondered about worker treatment for the organic, as well). How sustainable is this food I am eating?

It would be truly great if Ontario got an eco-labelling program. I really think it would be successful since, for me personally, my only hesitation with buying local is that it simply takes longer, and let's face it, sometimes you need that extra 60 seconds for something else. If there was an eco-label, not only would it be easy to pick out quickly which food to buy, it would likely lead some people to think about the issue – which they might not otherwise have done.

I hope that, by the time my student-budget days are behind me, an eco-label will exist in Ontario.

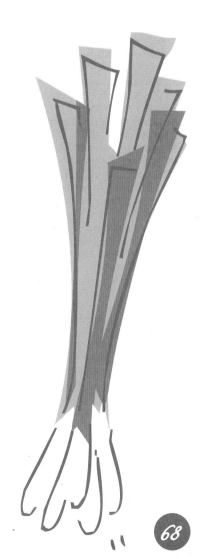

Food Charter Recipe

Add a willingness and plan to meet with various parts of society – municipal and provincial government, school districts, health regions, community–based organizations to have broad acceptance of the Food Charter.

Combine a capacity to follow through on getting commitments of groups and institutions to publicly support and enact elements of the Food Charter.

All these ingredients kneaded with determination, and leavened with the energy of community will incubate an alternative food system and make a Good Food Charter.

by Don Kossick

Packed with enthusiasm, energy, thought, different ingredients of the food cycle and those who produce and consume food, the Good Food Charter is a healthy, wholesome alternative to the industrial food system.

Ingredients
A strong portion of a wish to create an alternative food system.

Equal parts coming together of those who comprise the food cycle, rural and urban – producers, workers who process and distribute the food, eaters – citizens who consume food.

A thorough and participatory mixing process allowing for a full exchange of what an alternative food system would look like from the different points in the food cycle.

A collective agreement in full measure to adopt and accept a Food Charter that can work for everyone.

Stir in a deep desire for actions and activities that would achieve the realization of Food Charter goals.

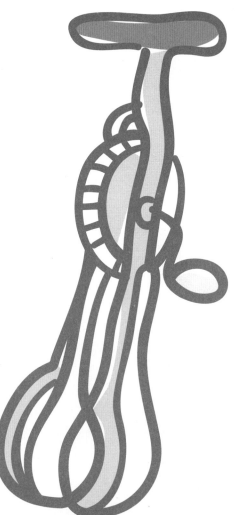

Working Towards a Just and Sustainable Food System in the City of Vancouver

Food Policy in Vancouver: A Short History

Discussions about the desirability of a coordinated food policy for the City of Vancouver have been taking place for over ten years. In 1990, nutritionists in the Vancouver Health Department initiated internal discussions about the need for a food policy. Issues discussed included local food security, the production and supply of adequate quality foods and people's ability to acquire them. Through local networking with other agencies, the nutritionists expanded their discussions to include agricultural land sustainability, the Buy BC First program, food support programs and nutrition education programs.

by Wendy Mendes

On July 8, 2003, Vancouver City Council approved a motion supporting the development of a just and sustainable food system for the City of Vancouver. A just and sustainable food system is one in which food production, processing, distribution and consumption are integrated to enhance the environmental, economic, social and nutritional health of a particular place. To provide leadership in achieving this goal, and to build on the work of the Vancouver Agreement Food Task Group, the Lower Mainland Food Coalition and other community groups, a Food Policy Task Force was initiated.

The Food Policy Task Force was made up of city councillors, a Vancouver School Board trustee, a Vancouver Board of Parks and Recreation commissioner, representatives from Vancouver Coastal Health and the Greater Vancouver Regional District (GVRD), as well as representatives from approximately 70 community groups, many of which had been developing and delivering food-related programs and services in Vancouver for over a decade. In striking the Food Policy Task Force, the goal of City Council was to recognize and build upon existing community experience and expertise.

By 1993, these meetings became formalized and the Vancouver Food Policy Coalition (VFPC) was created. Members included FarmFolk/CityFolk, Vancouver Health Department, City of Vancouver Social Planning Department, BC Ministry of Agriculture, Reach Community Health Centre, Chinese Cultural Centre, BC Dieticians and Nutritionists Association, the Greater Vancouver Food Bank Society and the Council of Marketing Boards for BC.

In August 1995, Vancouver's Medical Health Officer reported to City Council on the food policy discussions that had been taking place in the community, and plans for the future. In October of the same year, the Medical Health Officer informed City Council of the existence of the Vancouver Food Policy Coalition and their discussions about generating a food policy for the City of Vancouver. City Council received the report for information but no further city action was taken at the time.

In 1996, the functions of the Vancouver Health Department became a provincial responsibility. Even in the absence of a city-administered Health Department, discussions about community-based food policy initiatives continued. Much of the work took place under the auspices of the Vancouver Food Policy Coalition.

At the same time, a number of city-supported initiatives, including community gardens, farmers markets and emergency food programs, were on going.

Between 1996 and 2003, a wide range of community organizations continued to develop and deliver food-related programs and services in Vancouver. Some of these groups were members of the Lower Mainland Food Coalition (LMFC) which emerged in 2002, and to which groups and organizations concerned about food policy were invited. From this meeting, a core group came forward, made up of farmers, nutritionists, media, researchers and citizens working on food issues in the community. Some of these people were previous VFPC directors and most had worked in the food community for years. The LMFC received support and funding from Health Canada, the Vancouver Agreement Food Task Team and Growing Green.

The Vancouver Food Policy Task Force and Food Action Plan

Once the Council motion was passed in July 2003 and the Food Policy Task Force formed, the first of two consultation processes was initiated. The outcome of the first round of consultation was the formulation of a Food Action Plan. The Action Plan focussed on areas where City of Vancouver has the jurisdictional power to act. In recognition of the fact that many food system issues must be addressed on a regional basis (and in many cases beyond), opportunities for collaboration with other municipalities, levels of government and community stakeholders were identified. The Action Plan was made up of three components:

1. A recommendation to create a Vancouver Food Policy Council (VFPC)

2. An interim work plan including five action items:
> City-wide food system assessment
> Rooftop gardens
> Community gardens
> Farmers' markets
> Coordinated food processing
> and distribution facility for
> low-income citizens

3. An implementation support system (a recommendation to create two, full-time, dedicated, City staff positions to facilitate food system goals). The two positions are a permanent full-time Food Policy Coordinator and temporary two-year Food System Planner.

Outcomes

On December 11, 2003, Vancouver City Council approved the proposed Food Action Plan, pending 2004 budget decisions. On March 11, 2004, at the Standing Committee Meeting on City Services and Budgets, City Council voted to approve the expenditures associated with the Action Plan. Finally, on July 14, 2004, the Food Policy Task Force, as its final act, elected members of Vancouver's first municipally affiliated Food Policy Council. The Vancouver Food Policy Council met for the first time in September 2004 to develop a detailed work plan that integrates and builds upon the projects and goals identified in the Food Action Plan.

By early in 2005, the VPFC had identified a number of priority work areas including: a) creation of a food charter for the City of Vancouver, b) increased access to groceries for residents of Vancouver; c) creation of an institutional food purchasing policy, and d) development of a coordinated effort towards food recovery.

Lessons Learned

Over the course of the consultation processes culminating in City Council approval of the Action Plan, and subsequent work undertaken by the VFPC and food policy staff, a number of lessons have been learned about how to forge collaborative relationships between local government and community groups to achieve food-system goals. Some of these lessons include the following:

Lesson 1:
Build on Community Knowledge and Expertise

Much of Vancouver's collective success to date is directly linked to the expertise and experience of Task Force members in guiding the process and identifying needs and possible solutions.

Lesson 2:
Conduct Consultation Processes in Open and Democratic Manner
A number of Food Policy Task Force members indicated that they felt the collective formulation of the Food Action Plan and election of the Vancouver Food Policy Council were among the most democratic consultation processes in which they had ever taken part.

Lesson 3:
Build & Enhance Partnerships
A key reminder throughout the consultation processes was that some of the resources and policy tools necessary to address food-system issues fall outside the jurisdiction of some Canadian municipalities. Although the focus of the actions proposed by the Task Force was on those areas where the City of Vancouver has the capacity to act, attention was also given to identifying areas where collaboration with other levels of government, other municipalities and other community stakeholders would be necessary.

Lesson 4:
Adopt a Systems Approach to Food Issues
A systems approach assumes that connections between food issues is necessary to ensure the health and vitality of the food system as a whole, and it allows City departments both to see their own role in food policies and programs, and to recognize connections between their work and that of other departments and community groups.

Lesson 5:
Forge Connections between Food Policy and Existing City Policies
When Vancouver's Action Plan went forward to City Council for approval, the City Manager noted that the proposed plan reinforced a number of existing City policy and development goals, including, in particular, those relating to sustainability.

It was also noted that the implementation of the Food Action Plan would provide significant advances to upcoming City initiatives and commitments, including the 2010 Winter Olympics, the World Urban Forum 2006 and Habitat Plus 30 initiatives, all of which have strong sustainability agendas involving citizen engagement and community development. It was argued that as Vancouver takes centre stage during these important international events, the City has the opportunity to showcase leadership and innovation in the development of sustainable food practices. As such, a key lesson that should be taken into account by other local governments is to forge connections between food-policy goals and complementary City policy and development goals already in place, particularly those that enable partnerships between local government and community groups.

*This paper has been adapted from Mendes, W. (2004), Creating a Just and Sustainable Food System for the City of Vancouver. Cities Feeding People Workshop Paper, International Development Research Centre August 29 – September 2, 2004, Toronto. The original paper was produced with the kind support of the Cities Feeding People program of the International Development Research Centre.

Canada's Co-op Atlantic

Showing the Way to Cooperation amoung Cooperatives

by J.Tom Webb

For more than 75 years, Co-op Atlantic (CA) has linked Maritime farmer cooperatives and consumer retail cooperatives within a single structure. CA's combination of producer and consumer co-ops makes it unusual among co-ops, and well positioned against multinational competitors. CA's Agricultural Division has recently been a money earner for the organization and represents about 15-20% of annual volume, totalling several hundred million dollars. And with its new "agro-food strategy,"using its mix of farmer and consumer members to forge new business links, CA may be showing the way for cooperation among cooperatives around the world.

Context of the Agro-Food Strategy

The emerging and evolving strategy is a new set of products and labels that promote local production, food 'traceability,' and trust. The brands link the consumer retail system with producers and producer cooperatives in a growing network of cooperation.

CA's new strategy takes on one of the major problems facing cooperatives in the rapidly globalizing economy: the triple whammy of corporate concentration, horizontal diversification and vertical integration. The impact is perhaps greater in the English-speaking world, where the consumer-led thrust of cooperative business has tended to produce "cooperative silos." Each form of cooperative–housing, retail electric, funeral, insurance, and credit unions–is like a self-contained silo, focussed on its own business sector. They have generally limited cooperation among cooperatives to fraternal links. They have done very little business with each other, sometimes preferring to have more business-like dealings with traditional corporate businesses that ask no favours.

This has left cooperatives without many of the economies of scale enjoyed by their competitors. Compared to horizontally diversified competitors, cooperatives have also been more vulnerable when a particular industry got into trouble. A major Co-op Atlantic competitor, Sobeys, is involved in real estate development, car rentals, fish processing, manufacturing and many other diverse ventures; the other multinational competitor is even more diversified.

Co-ops increasingly find themselves facing enormous competitors able to exert growing influence and sometimes control over not just the marketplace but global suppliers as well. On the other side of the coin, because co-ops are community-based, cooperative members and the public expect them to be more supportive of local business and community than their competitors.

Beef about Beef

The Co-op Atlantic agro-food strategy began with the problems facing beef farmers in Atlantic Canada. Atlantic beef lacked a strong positive consumer image compared to beef from western Canada. An honest assessment would have conceded that Atlantic beef was inconsistent in quality. The preferred beef on consumer cooperative shelves came from western Canada.

As part of its business, CA sold feed grains to beef and other livestock producers. The CA structure allowed an opportunity for the mutual interests of consumers and farmers to override their conflicting interests, and Atlantic Tender Beef Classic was born. The resulting cooperative business deal was pure mutual self-help.

How Does it Work?

Farmers agree to use specified stock quality, feeding regimes and animal care, and to purchase high-quality feed mixes from Co-op Atlantic. CA in turn agrees to purchase all the beef farmers produce and to feature and promote it in co-op stores as premium quality beef. Each cow can be traced back to the calf, and the feed from Co-op Atlantic contains no animal byproducts or renderings.

This approach was so successful with beef that farmers and Co-op Atlantic quickly expanded the product mix to chicken and pork, rebranded as Atlantic Tender Meats. Nor did it end there. Co-op Atlantic then created the Market Town house brand, with items ranging from potatoes "further subdivided into those best for baking, boiling or fries" to peanut butter, and including apple pies made by a family firm using apples from a cooperative. As with Atlantic Tender Meats, these products are sourced locally.

To make this happen required the creation of complex sets of partnerships involving marketing boards, government agricultural agencies in four provinces, the member retail cooperatives that make up Co-op Atlantic, the newly formed beef cooperative, secondary processors who manufacture the 'Market Town' and private label products, plus independent farmers and their associations.

Co-op Atlantic did not wade into this based on hunches and hopes. They used a strong and growing e-flyer subscription list to determine if Atlantic Canadians were interested in what could be offered. Response to the e-survey was very strong: from 8300 weekly e-flyer subscribers, Co-op Atlantic received almost 2900 responses in less than 30 hours, along with 50 pages of comments from members and subscribers. It was clear from the research and the partnership discussions that the cooperative system enjoys a privileged position of trust with those producers and processors as well as among members and consumers. They trusted cooperatives to provide quality, safe food and to 'do the right thing.'

Traceability Is Key

Food safety and ethical production have become real and present issues with consumers, including animal treatment, additives, pesticides, fertilizers, GMOs, e-coli and privatization of water. The recent move by the US government to pass an anti-bioterrorism act to protect food from chemical and biological tampering has heightened awareness among North American consumers on a wide range of food issues. Consumers increasingly want to know, for both primary and secondary products, who grows their food, what happens to it chemically and mechanically and its source. They want to know what an animal was fed and its health record. Increasingly, consumers want 'traceability.'

Survey respondents also made it clear they like locally produced goods from people they can reach and trust and that they associate such products with freshness, community well-being and a sense of self-sufficiency. Members and consumers also have more faith that local products were not produced with health and safety risks to farmers and farm workers and that production involved a living wage. These concerns are not held by everyone, but the extent to which they are held is surprising and growing.

Co-op Atlantic allocated a significant part of its marketing effort to promotion. Beef was the lead item on many flyers for much of 2002 and beyond. Local producers were featured in flyer banners. CA produced a television brand ad and branded grocery bags.

The potatoes came in smaller packages, with clear identification on what each variety is suited for along with cooking instructions, nutritional information and recipes. Providing information about each type of potato changed the way members and shoppers bought potatoes. The lowly potato went from being a standard commodity to being a value-added product. Brand signage and additional flyer activity, featuring price coupons, was supplemented with complimentary products to encourage trial and awareness.

Learning from the Co-op Atlantic Example

The Co-op Atlantic agro-food strategy (as well as fair trade initiatives in the UK, US, and elsewhere) provides food for thought and hope for what the future might be. Consumer concerns about food quality and safety, their trust of cooperative businesses and the challenge of multinational growth, taken together represent a daunting threat and an exciting opportunity. One can imagine an international cooperative purchasing system that, while encouraging local and cooperative procurement, has the resources to create ecological, health, safety and social justice standards for food products and the strength to ensure that suppliers meet those standards. One can picture international cooperative brands reflecting cooperative values and principles and applying them in a thoughtful way that people trust. One can envisage new cooperative-to-cooperative business relationships based on openness and trust.

This article first appeared in the *Cooperative Grocer* - a trade magazine for consumer food cooperatives www.cooperativegrocer.coop.

Green Thumbs / Growing Kids

*Healthy Eating & Healthy
Ecosystems in a School
Community Garden*
by Sunday Harrison

Our project involves children in a neighbourhood with the highest population density in North America, called St. Jamestown, and the adjacent community, a mixed-income and highly diverse neighbourhood called Cabbagetown. The school draws from both communities, which have in common a lack of green space. The language and cultural groups are probably the most diverse of anywhere in Canada.

With 38% of the total food-bank users in Canada, Ontario has more than its share of hungry people. Studies have shown that babies born in St. Jamestown have lower birth weights than average. Rents in St. Jamestown skyrocketed when some of the buildings were taken over by private companies and now more people than ever before cannot afford to eat properly. Often the culturally familiar foods are not available in the neighbourhood or are only available at inflated prices. With many parents working extra shifts to pay the rent, the quality of food in the home may have dropped. Local schools may have Student Nutrition Programs.

However, school board cutbacks to lunchroom supervision has placed more stress on the ability of school-based feeding programs to adequately monitor children's food intake.

Our project began in 1999 as an after-school gardening and nature program for children 6-12 years old. Children learn to garden and participate in food production as well as ecosystem restoration. In 2001 we got involved with the school garden project as well, and began gardening programs at both sites.

Since we began, children's diets are getting more attention as obesity and diabetes among children reach epidemic levels. Clearly, children are not eating enough fresh fruits and vegetables, and are getting too many empty calories from cheap fast foods. There are many dimensions to this problem, and one of them is that some children do not have a taste for the healthy choices because they have not been properly exposed to them. Parents often do not realize that a food may need to be offered up to ten times until it is accepted. Many children prefer their vegetables and fruits raw and simple, not mixed or cooked or dressed, as they are often presented.

When children see the food growing in the garden, you can see the paradigm shift take place before your eyes. The disbelief gives way to excitement as they exclaim, is that a REAL tomato? As they are encouraged to water or spread compost near the plant's roots, their role changes from consumer to producer, from the nurtured to the nurturer–and with this shift comes both power and responsibility! This completes a conceptual circle normally broken by the marketplace, a circle we take so much for granted we have forgotten it even exists.

In addition to offering the chance to harvest produce, the school garden serves as a location for families to meet and share recipes, fostering cross-cultural interaction. Universal yet diverse, national cuisines and family recipes are a source of pride in one's heritage, no matter in what economic circumstances the family finds itself. Thus there is a strong link to emotional and mental health in the garden.

A 11,000 square foot area on the school ground became available after portable classrooms were removed, due to declining enrolment. Residents on the two facing streets were mobilized by a local entrepreneur to support a naturalized garden, and the school garden began in 2000 with the planting of native grasses and perennial flowering plants. An area was left for vegetable production. Green Thumbs/Growing Kids gained funding support to install a composter, bring vermicomposting into the school and begin conditioning the soil for vegetable production. A fence was required to keep dogs out of the food-growing area. By 2002, the native plants had filled in the meadow and the cultivated area was beginning to support food production.

We get classrooms to start and look after seedlings (mainly tomatoes and peppers) in the classroom under lights. This ties in well with Ontario's Grade 3 curriculum, although other grades have been involved. Beginning in May, the classes come outside for a transplanting workshop, and the young children plant peas and beans, staggering the planting so that harvest will be staggered as well. In 2003 and 2004, the compost-enhanced beds began to yield high quantities of quality foods. We (GT/GK) are, in fact two single moms whose children attended this school, so we were also involved in the school council and helped to start a Nutrition/Environment Committee that supported the introduction of the Salad Bar concept into the already-nutritious Hot Lunch program there.

The Salad Bar allows children the choice of a variety of fresh fruits and vegetables, along with carbohydrate and protein choices. Children serve themselves and learn to take what they really will eat. It has been very successful, both in terms of increasing the children's nutrition but also bringing staff and parents into the lunchroom, buying lunch and supporting the program.

And since the Salad Bar generates more food scraps for the compost, we're in a positive cycle of having more wet waste to compost and build soil life on the school ground. The garden in turn supports the Salad Bar, and children bring the produce from the garden into the lunchroom.

To maximize the produce available for children, we have concentrated on growing plants that a) mature in September and keep fresh in the garden until December; and b) produce copious amounts of small fruits, such as cherry tomatoes, beans, peas. We also concentrate on offering summer programs in the school garden so that children and families can access the bounty.

We think this is the key to the success of school gardens in Canada. Our growing season just cannot exclude July and August as a prime time to be in the garden. Some schools even have greenhouses and could extend the season in both directions, but even with season extenders there's just so much to enjoy about the summer garden. Community groups, particularly children's service agencies and family programs, are natural clients for the summer programs.

We offer programs three days per week, staggered so that there's plenty of produce, and integrate the programming with environmental education via composting and arts and crafts activities in the naturalized meadow. Two of the programs include cooking in the garden with the families. We run our summer programs before or after the heat of the day—mornings and evenings. The programs include replanting as well, ensuring continuous produce through the fall.

The compost is an integral part of nutrition programming in the garden. It teaches the design of a closed, zero-waste system, fosters biodiversity, sequesters carbon, reduces fossil fuel use, and raises the humus level of the garden soil, "feeding" the plants that feed us. It is simple to maintain, once the process is understood. By using the compost in programming, we maximize its educational value along with its intrinsic value.

Vermicomposting illustrates a habitat as well, and produces a high-quality product that ultimately could be sold.

We have lots of opportunities in the garden programming to discuss, with children and adults alike, the benefits of local food, slow food and organic food. We take a non-judgemental position regarding organic food, simply encouraging children and parents to fully wash non-organic produce to remove pesticide residues, as it has been shown that these are harmful especially to children. We'd rather see you buy a local apple or potato conventionally grown than an organic one from California. Of course, we use no chemicals in our gardens, practising companion planting, organic pest controls and simply more compost for any problems we encounter.

The spirit and essence of this program is child-centred and holistic. Even the very youngest can participate. As a safe and healthy space for young children outdoors, the school garden becomes a meeting place for parents and caregivers to relax and share a laugh. Older children benefit from the hands-on experience and the opportunity to observe nature's cycles daily and weekly rather than just on field trips or holidays. The challenge lies in obtaining funding for initiatives like ours because what we do falls outside the traditional health and education system.

The Bean Keepers Story
by Jane Hayes

Not long ago in a town named Tumbleweed there was a terrible drought. One year, it hardly rained in May. It hardly rained in June and July, and it didn't rain at all in August.

When fall came, the farmers harvested the scrawny crops. The adults were worried. "What if there's no rain next year?" asked Ms Krauss, the kindergarten teacher. "We won't have enough food," said farmer Elijah Bernstein. "Not enough beans, that's for sure," said farmer Joe Piper.

Paolo overheard the adults. He met his friends at their treehouse and told them what was going on. Ellie had a bright idea. "We could grow food," she said. "But what do we know how to grow?" asked Olivia. "I know how to grow beans," said little Maria, who had grown them with Ms Krauss in kindergarten that year. "Yeah! We grew beans at school, too," said Jim, Charlie, and Ellie.

"Let's make a list of what we need to grow beans," said Olivia, who liked to make lists. Jim thought of the first thing, and Olivia wrote it down in her best printing:

1. Get beans.

They stopped the list there, which made Olivia a little grumpy, and went in search of beans. Paolo's mom gave him pinto beans from the cupboard. Ellie's dad gave her kidney beans from a jar in the pantry. Charlie got green bush beans from his garden.

The next day, they met at the tree house to look at their beans. The kidney beans and pinto beans were dry, but the green beans were still fresh, and the seeds inside looked very small and too soft to be planted. "We need more beans," said Jim. "We need dry beans," added Ellie. Olivia wrote on her list:

2. Get a lot more beans.

3. Get dry beans.

"What will we do when we get a lot more beans?" wondered Maria. "How will we tell them apart?" Paolo suggested they put them in paper bags and write the name of the bean on the bag. Olivia wrote on the list:

4. Put beans in paper bags. Label bags (bean name, where from).

They went looking for more beans. Elijah Bernstein gave Paolo scarlet runner beans. "Sometimes these grow 20 feet high!" he said. Charlie went to Tumbleweed's community garden and found string beans, yellow beans, and waxed beans that had dried on their beanstalks. Olivia asked Ming Pi for some of his special Chinese long beans. "Each bean grows three feet long," said Ming Pi proudly. Ms Krauss gave Ellie some rattlesnake snap beans and said, "Please give me a few back if you grow extras so I can grow them with the kindergarten class next year."

Little Maria's uncle gave her black turtle beans and some Mexican jumping beans. "Why do they jump?" asked Maria. "The jumping bean has a little worm that lives inside. When it wiggles, the bean jumps up and down," he explained.

He gave her special orca beans too. "They look like an orca whale if you squint just right," he said.

One day, they visited Joe Piper, Tumbleweed's famous bean farmer. He'd been growing beans forever. Joe Piper listened to what they were up to and said, "Well, at last. Until you walked in the door, I thought I was Tumbleweed's only Bean Keeper. I've been one since I was knee high to a beanstalk. All my friends were too. Truth is, I'm getting a little old to be the only Bean Keeper now, so I'm very glad you're here to help. Do you know that Bean Keepers have an important job to do?"

"What? What's our job?" Olivia and Jim asked in unison. "Each year you have to plant beans, water them, and pick some for growing next year after they've dried on the vine," said Joe Piper. "That sounds like what we're doing, only we hadn't figured out how we were going to do it," said Charlie.

"Do you have any beans for us?" asked Ellie. Joe Piper rolled up his sleeves and went deep into his cupboards. He pulled out paper bag after paper bag of beans until the bags were piled so high that they had to stand on chairs to see the top of the pile. Joe Piper gave them some beans from each bag and labelled each one. "Welcome to the Bean Keepers," said Joe Piper. "Don't forget that you can eat some too!" he added. "Thanks, Joe!" they said as they waved goodbye. "We'll do our best to be good Bean Keepers, we promise!"

Back at the tree house, Olivia added to their list:

5. Plant beans.
6. Water beans.
7. Let beans dry (on the vine).
8. Pick beans.
9. Eat some of the beans!

Spring was still a few months away. They skated and waited. They drank hot chocolate and waited. They hung out in the treehouse and waited. One day Paolo said, "Let's do a play about the Bean Keepers for the talent show." Jim said,

"We can invite all the kids to help us grow the beans!"

They turned their list into a rap song for the show. They practised and practised and finally the talent show night came. "Announcing the Bean Keepers!" said Paolo. Olivia shouted, "Bean Keepers always use a list to help them, now let's rap it!" They rapped:

"Want to be a Bean Keeper? This is how.
Get beans into paper bags, then label.
Wait, wait, wait till spring.
Plant beans into the soil, then water.
Wait, wait, wait till fall.
Pick beans off the vine.
Wait, wait, wait till they dry.
Get beans into paper bags, then label.
Wait, wait, wait till spring.
Want to be a Bean Keeper?
Now you know how.
So don't wait, wait, wait at all!"

The applause was deafening! Ms Krauss announced that they had won the talent show and that her class would help from now on. Dozens of other kids said they'd help, too.

Paolo, Ellie, Jim, Olivia, Maria and Charlie spent the final weeks before spring distributing the beans among all the new Bean Keepers. Finally the soil warmed up, the trees began to leaf out, and Joe Piper said, "It is time to plant the beans. Plant them close to your houses so you remember to water them." Everyone got busy planting.

It was another year of hardly any rain. Early in June, Joe Piper said, "Time to mulch your beans. Put straw around them. That way they need less water."

In July, Ellie had a great idea. "Let's grow the beans with leftover bath water." They convinced everyone in Tumbleweed to plug their tubs when they showered. They collected water in buckets and carried it to the beans.

The beans grew and grew. Finally fall came.

The kids collected their beans, put them in paper bags, labelled them and gathered together. "Each of my waxed beans made 150 more beans," said Charlie. "My scarlet runner beans and my orca beans are really beautiful," said Paolo. "My Chinese long beans are over three feet long," said Olivia. Everyone had a story to tell.

They invited Joe Piper to see the beans they had grown. "You kids are spectacular Bean Keepers. You've grown over 100 pounds of beans during a terrible drought year. You ought to show Mayor Emma Jones," he suggested.

Mayor Jones couldn't believe what she saw. "You've grown more beans than most of you weigh! Let's celebrate with a bean festival!" "Could we put on our play at the bean festival?" asked Maria. "Absolutely! We'll invite schools from other towns to come too so they can learn how to be Bean Keepers," said the mayor.

School kids came to the bean festival from all around. Elijah Bernstein and Ms Krauss couldn't stop talking about the Bean Keepers. Paolo, Charlie, Jim, Olivia, Ellie and Maria put on their show again.

Olivia even printed up the rap song and a new version of the list and handed them out to everyone who came. Old Joe Piper just smiled. There would be Bean Keepers aplenty for years to come.

The Bean Keepers Pilot Project

Evergreen (www.evergreen.ca) and Seeds of Diversity Canada (www.seeds.ca) are working with schools to protect the diversity of beans and other heritage seeds. There are over 2000 types of beans being grown in Canada and the majority are rare. Imagine that 2000 of the 16,000 schools in Canada grow and care for one type of bean each!

Through the Bean Keepers project, schools are invited to read the Bean Keeper's story, to grow and save bean seeds, and to send a few seeds back to Seeds of Diversity for safekeeping in its public heritage seed bank.

To sign up, contact Evergreen at: jhayes@evergreen.ca, 1-888-426-3138 x 227 or visit www.evergreen.ca/eng/lg/bean-keepers.html.

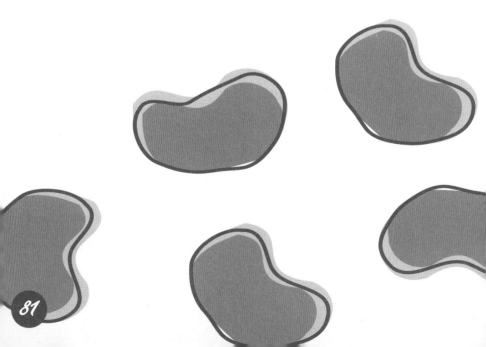

Growing Food Security in Alberta

Enthusiastic and Committed People Making a Difference!
by Susan Roberts and Angie Dedrick

The Growing Food Security in Alberta (GFSA) is an exciting project focussed on enhancing the health of impoverished children in Alberta. It is built on previous work in Alberta conducted at the Putting Food First workshop hosted by Dietitians of Canada and the Provincial Nutritionist's Food Security Network (PNFSN) of Alberta in May 2002. The workshop identified a keen stakeholder interest in building a food security network in Alberta. The GFSA gathered further support through the development of a Food Security Tool Kit in 2002. The Tool Kit is a set of resources that provide support to actively engage citizens in building food security–this tool kit has since been placed on the GFSA Web site at www.foodsecurityalberta.ca. In 2002 the PNFSN also guided an environmental scan of food security initiatives in Alberta, which served as the connector to those involved in food security in Alberta.

Funding through Public Health Agency of Canada (PHAC) Population Health Fund (November 2002- March 2005) facilitated the formation and coordination of an environmental scan that built from the 2002 scan and served as the 'launching pad'

for making the provincial food security network a reality. A broad sector steering committee, including individuals working with Aboriginal communities, food banks, private sector, school boards, as well as a rancher, policy experts, health promotion specialists, a public member from a remote Alberta community and community nutritionists, have guided the initiative.

The network focusses on fostering awareness of food security as a health issue and its impact on the health of children, among members of the public, community organizations, health care workers, government departments and the business community.

The GFSA provincial Food Security Network includes members of the public, groups, organizations and people who are keenly interested. It has been built on information and contacts from the comprehensive GFSA environmental scan conducted in March 2003 and the GFSA Social Marketing Plan.

Our Vision
All children and families in Alberta have healthy food

Our Mission
Engaging Albertans–groups, organizations, business, governments and individuals–in strategies to ensure secure access to adequate amounts of safe, nutritious, culturally appropriate food for everyone, produced in an environmentally sustainable way and provided in a manner that promotes human dignity. (Adapted from OPHA Food Security Workgroup 2002.)

The GFSA Network has many unique qualities:

• The network and the Web site provide links to resources, groups and Web sites, and a means for communication and suggestions on how to become involved in GFSA and the network.

• Key Groups and Contacts:
AB Food Bank Network Association, Alberta Public Health Association,

Alberta Food Producers Association, Alberta Urban Municipality Association, Alberta Teachers Association, Alberta Healthy Living Network, Alberta School Boards Association, Family and Community Support Services, Western Grocers, Canadian Prenatal Nutrition Program, contacts from the "Survey of Food Security Initiatives" and participants in the "Putting Food First" workshop.

• The GFSA Social Marketing Plan has helped build awareness of food security in Alberta. It promotes the GFSA Network and its activities, and engages Albertans in solutions. Target audiences include: school boards, Family and Child Social Services, Agriculture, the health regions, food writers and politicians. Presentations across the province and Canada and a new Video in 2005 reinforce the GFSA key messages:

• Food security is an issue for everyone.

• Our food choices have a profound effect on our community.

• There are lots of opportunities to get involved in food security.

• We want to use creative solutions to achieve food security.

• The GFSA in partnership with others across the province organized a Conference Reality Check 2005, Spring 2005. The conference was a huge success and has been a vehicle for capacity building and information sharing among groups and individuals affected by or working with food security.

• The GFSA has an evaluation strategy that includes three logic models accompanying survey tools and a plan for collecting data on success indicators for the project.

• The GFSA policy agenda is being developed to guide the policy-related advocacy work of the GFSA Policy group. The GFSA steering committee collaborated on a letter in response to the proposed regulation changes on the Employment Support Act and Housing,

and developed an election Backgrounder for the Alberta election November 2005. Both are available on the GFSA Web site.

What is notable about the GFSA initiative?
We have made some progress.

• GFSA has a hard-working and diverse steering committee–people who have given their time and energy and are from the many facets and perspectives of food security.

• GFSA has been informed through research and practice.

• GFSA has developed three logic models to inform the practice and policy development for the Steering Committee, Network and Community.

What does GFSA have to share?
Energy, enthusiasm, and more.

• A Web site with a list-serv, many resources and links, including a Power Point presentation and a Web-steamed video (March 2005).

• Links to Albertans and others from across Canada who are GFSA Network participants willing to share experiences and resources from all spectrums of food security–community gardens, school food policy, community shared agriculture, buying local, collective kitchens, etc.

• A new GFSA video that will build awareness of food security in Alberta and beyond (available March 2005).

• An opportunity to share learning and learn from each other.

What Lessons did GFSA Learn?

• Anyone can be a part – food security is everyone's business.

• Building an effective and active network takes time and resources.

• Personal one-on-one in-person or phone conversations are the best vehicles for building the relationships key to creating a network.

• A Web site is useful for resource and information sharing, but in-person or phone contact builds a network that spawns activity and action.

For more information contact us at info@foodsecurityalberta.ca or visit the Web Site at www.foodsecurityalberta.ca.

Kamloops Food Policy Council

Leading the Way in Grassroots Food Action
by Laura Kalina and Julie Johnson

With the adoption of a Food and Nutrition Policy Framework in 2000 at both the municipal and health region levels, the Kamloops Food Policy Council (KFPC) has moved along the food security continuum to make nutritious food more available in the community. The mission of KFPC is to promote local food action while developing food policy that will address the underlying issues of food insecurity. This article will highlight the food and nutrition policy framework and two projects that have spawned as a result: the Gardengate Training Centre and Kamloops FoodShare.

In October 2000, the Thompson Health Region adopted the following four elements for their Food and Nutrition Policy:

• Safe and nutritious food is available within the region for all residents.

• Access to the safe and nutritious food is not limited by economic status, location or other factors beyond a resident's control.

• There is a local and regional agriculture and food production system that supplies wholesome food to the region's residents on a sustainable basis.

• All residents have the information and skills to achieve nutritional well-being.

The KFPC was excited about formalizing the food policy because it provided a framework to guide the decision-making process and subsequent action plan.

People often wonder about the impact of a food and nutrition policy. Well, if you were walking through a city with a food security policy, you might see things like:

• a farmer's market in a central location

• fruit trees and edible plants in the parks

• a public transportation system that gets people easily from low-income areas to food stores

• market gardens and farms as green space

• comfortable places for mothers to breastfeed

• accessible nutrition education programs

The goal of the KFPC is to work with local governments, community groups and individuals to implement this food and nutrition policy at the local level. An excellent example of policy implementation is the creation of the Gardengate Training Centre. Land was needed to develop the Gardengate Training Centre and the food policy provided the necessary support to secure the land. Once the land was secured, in-kind support and funding were obtained to develop the training programs.

What Is the Gardengate Training Centre?
Gardengate includes an organic production garden, greenhouse and training facility on two acres of land owned by the Interior Health (formerly called Thompson Health Region) in Kamloops. Gardengate was developed to address the issue of food security at its core by providing land and training for people to learn to grow their own food.

This innovative horticulture project aims to develop knowledge and skills to enhance access to healthy food and employment for people with mental health disabilities. In addition, as part of building community capacity, over 20,000 pounds of produce from Gardengate was donated to emergency food outlets last year.

Gardengate is a partnership project between the Kamloops Food Policy Council and the BC society of Training for Health and Employment Opportunities (THEO BC) and is funded by Interior Health, Mental Health programs. Many other groups are involved, such as the Kamloops Food Bank & Food Action Centre, University College of the Caribou's Horticulture Program, Ministry of Agriculture, North Shore Business Association, Community Gardens and community volunteers.

Kamloops FoodShare

In an effort to further implement the policy and make nutritious food more available to the marginalized members of our community, the Kamloops FoodShare project was created. Our mission statement is More Food, Less Waste, Efficient Delivery. Our goal is to increase access to nutritious food for all people. We pick up and deliver large quantities of good food that is currently being discarded. Recovered food is then quickly distributed to non-profit agencies that provide meals for people.

FoodShare is based in the Kamloops Food Action Centre and is administered by a working group of provincial, municipal, private-sector and non-profit stakeholders who have a vested interest in food security. The working group provides direct input into the development and operation of the program, so that all aspects of food donations are addressed. These stakeholders also contribute money or in-kind products and services to the development of FoodShare, and are dedicated to the success of the program. This makes FoodShare a true community endeavour!

We partner with agencies that already have vehicles on the road, picking up their own donations. These agencies provide the use of their vehicles and drivers for FoodShare deliveries on a dispatch system. When drivers pick up food that is specifically for the FoodShare program, they keep that food separate and then deliver it to all the agencies that are scheduled to receive food that day.

The advantage to this group approach is twofold. First, it lessens the workload for donors because they now deal with one central contact that serves many agencies, as opposed to coordinating with the numerous agencies in town. Second, many agencies previously ran their own vehicles and paid their own staff to do the same thing that others were already doing. FoodShare coordinates all these efforts to make it convenient for donors and efficient for agencies.

As the central coordinating body for food donation pick-ups and deliveries, Kamloops FoodShare does the following:

- solicit food donations
- pick up, store and deliver food to non-profit agencies
- field donation requests/offers
- ensure food-safe practices through training and monitoring
- market our services
- develop toolkits
- track and compile food-related statistics
- maintain good relationships among all stakeholders by coordinating regular meetings and opportunities for feedback

As the only food recovery program in BC outside Vancouver, we hope to lead the way for other communities to develop similar programs. The benefits of FoodShare extend even beyond food security. Crime prevention, health promotion and waste reduction are other positive results that FoodShare cultivates.

With the development of FoodShare, economic development opportunities have also arisen. Part of the FoodShare program is a gleaning focus, especially in the summer months.

The fruit and vegetables that are gleaned can be dehydrated and packaged into soup mixes and snacks, and then sold as a fundraiser or social enterprise business venture.

During the first week of operations in January 2005, FoodShare recovered over 1500 pounds of food, mostly produce (that's 9000 servings of fruits and veggies)! In the first month, we increased our donor base and agency recipients by over 200%. With the support of the City of Kamloops, Interior Health Authority, retail community and non-profit agencies, we are sure to enjoy a successful first year of operations!

The Kamloops Food Policy Council has been working along the food security continuum for over a decade. From the start of community kitchens in 1989 to community gardens, Gardengate Training Centre and Food Policy development, we are working in partnership with many community groups to make nutritious and healthy food available to all. For more information on Kamloops and other successful projects, check out *Building Food Security in Canada: From Hunger to Sustainable Food Systems: A Community Guide*, 2nd edition available through laura@kamloopsfoodshare.org.

Winnipeg Regional Health Authority Home Care Program

The following is a snapshot of the topics discussed in each of the four training modules.

Module 1:
Safe Food Handling and Tasks of Home Support (Cooking, Laundry, Cleaning)

Topics include: common sources of food-borne illness, preventing food-borne illness in the home, cross-contamination, proper cooking and food storage, safe food-handling techniques and proper hand-washing techniques.

Module 2:
Canada's Food Guide and Special Diets

Topics include: principles of healthy eating through review of Canada's Food Guide, 24-hour food recall, role of vitamins and minerals, use of supplements, and special diets (with focus on diabetes and heart disease).

Module 3:
Cooking I

Topics include: basic principles of food preparation, basic recipe preparation and common ingredient usage.

Module 4:
Cooking II

Topics include: meal planning, cooking with consideration to special diets and cultural and religious food practices.

Reassessment of DSS Knowledge
At the end of each Module 4 class, direct service staff (DSS) are asked to complete a general knowledge questionnaire. This is the same questionnaire that was completed by DSS in the fall of 2000. The readministration of the general knowledge questionnaire has provided the opportunity to measure the impact the module training program has had on the knowledge level of DSS. Overall, the increase in knowledge that has been seen as a result of the module training program has been encouraging.

Making Nutritious and Culturally Appropriate Foods Available to Clients
by Kristin Hildahl

The Winnipeg Regional Health Authority (WRHA) Home Care program strives to make nutritious and culturally appropriate foods more readily accessible to Home Care clients through a number of initiatives. In May of 2002, a modular training program was launched for direct service staff within the WRHA Home Care program. The modular training program is mandatory staff education for all WRHA Home Care Attendants and Home Support Staff, and consists of facilitated education sessions and cooking classes. These training sessions promote the role that good nutrition plays in health and emphasize the importance of respecting the cultural and religious traditions of others. The importance of nutritious foods is emphasized through explanations of Canada's Food Guide and the role that it plays in optimizing health and well-being. The module training program also emphasizes food safety to ensure that Home Care clients have access to safe, secure foods.

Improvements have been seen in all areas, and the program strives to further these improvements.

In 2006, a survey of Home Care clients is planned to determine whether client satisfaction with meal preparation has improved as a result of the DSS modular training program.

Another initiative the Home Care program has undertaken to improve food security is the development of a Meal Preparation Resource Guide for DSS to use when preparing meals for clients. This resource, published in the spring of 2003, is provided to all WRHA Home Care Attendants and Home Support Staff. The Meal Preparation Resource Guide provides access to healthy meal plans, recipes that can be used in client situations and recipes/techniques that may be appropriate in special circumstances (e.g. ethnic situations).

The Meal Preparation Resource Guide helps to diminish a potential barrier that these service providers may face when entering unfamiliar situations, such as ethnic situations, preparing kosher diets, etc. As well, this resource can be used by DSS as a tool for planning meals with clients and thus help in the development of healthy eating habits. When people plan what they are going to eat, the attitude towards eating often improves, thus potentially leading to improved health and well-being. Home Care clients can benefit from a greater variety of foods due to use of this resource by Home Care staff, as staff now have easy access to a wide variety of recipes. This may also contribute to improvement in the overall health of clients. The program anticipates that implementation of the Meal Preparation Resource Guide will result in an increased level of client satisfaction with meal preparation, thus increasing the potential for the development of a positive relationship between clients and staff.

The Meal Preparation Resource Guide includes information on time management in the kitchen, what to do with leftovers, substitutions, hand washing, bulk meal preparation, appropriate food storage, appropriate thawing and freezing methods,

sanitizing solutions and tips on washing dishes. The Meal Preparation Resource Guide includes recipes for common breakfast, lunch and supper meals, recipes that may be found in eight different ethnic traditions commonly seen in the Home Care client population– Aboriginal/First Nations, Asian, Central European, Eastern European, Indian, Latin America/ Caribbean, Northern European and Southern European–and information on appropriate food preparation techniques regarding Jewish, Muslim, Hindu, Buddhist and Christian food practices. The section on kosher diets was produced through consultation with a rabbi at a local synagogue. As well, the resource provides information on vegetarian diets, healthy eating for older adults, definitions of common food-preparation terms and basic kitchen equipment, abbreviations, food equivalents and metric/imperial conversions. This comprehensive resource provides DSS with the tools They need to provide their clients with safe, nutritious and culturally appropriate foods.

The WRHA has a strong focus on sharing of information and resources. The Meal Preparation Resource Guide is available to other organizations and health authorities for a nominal fee.

In conclusion, the WRHA Home Care program's development of the module training program and the Meal Preparation Resource Guide for use by Home Care direct service staff has improved food security issues that may affect Home Care clients in the community. Direct service staff have evaluated the training program positively and the planned 2006 client evaluation will yield valuable data about client satisfaction with the quality, variety and cultural appropriateness of meals prepared by staff.

Kids in the Kitchen

Building Skills to Promote Food Security
by Joyce Slater

The tripling of obesity rates in Canadian children over the last 20 years is a disturbing trend. Paradoxically, many of these children come from families living in poverty who experience food insecurity. Community groups working with children often feel overwhelmed when trying to address this growing issue. We know promoting good nutrition is essential but this is not enough. Food security includes knowing how to prepare safe, healthy food. With the fast pace of life and the abundance of packaged, processed foods, many families and children have fewer opportunities to learn how to prepare their own food from scratch. Children are often home alone after school, preparing their own snacks and meals, and rely on packaged convenience foods.

The main idea behind Kids in the Kitchen is to teach kids about basic foods, healthy eating and food safety. The Kids in the Kitchen project grew out of two Kids' Cooking Clubs in Winnipeg plus a desire on the part of a handful of community nutritionists to make this activity available in as many community settings as possible. The end result was an interactive nutrition program for children ages 6-11, complete with a Community

Action Kit including a How-To manual and (almost) everything needed to start a Kids' Cooking Club:

• Kids in the Kitchen manual, with 21 lesson plans that include low-cost recipes and nutrition activities for groups of 12 children or less

• Sample forms and letters for funders, parents and community partners

• Aprons, measuring spoons and cups, most of the teaching resources required for the nutrition activities

Three hundred kits were distributed (for a nominal fee) in Manitoba to a variety of community-based organizations including Family Resource Centres, Brownie troupes, schools, Boys and Girls Clubs, First Nation organizations and community clubs. Kids in the Kitchen was created to provide a foundation for lifelong healthy eating through the following objectives:

• Provide opportunities for children to improve their food preparation skills

• Teach children healthy nutrition practices in a fun manner

• Give children the opportunity to learn about foods from different cultures

• Improve social supports for children

• Enhance community partnerships related to the issue of child health

• Encourage food security through promotion of affordable meal and snack ideas

• Make it easy for community leaders to implement a Kids' Cooking Club in their community

Kids in the Kitchen also provides opportunities for children to enhance math, gross motor, literacy and social skills. Here's what some community groups who have used Kids in the Kitchen had to say:

"The manual was great – it really helped. The cooking program was fun, we all learned a lot from it."

"It's really fun – I learned a lot."

"Kids are now dropping by and asking; 'Is the program still on? When will it be s tarting up again?'"

"We're teaching the children cooking skills and healthy habits. They are simple, healthy recipes they can make on their own if they have the ingredients at home."

Community organizations interested in starting their own cooking club can create their own Community Action Kit. A copy of the manual can be downloaded from: Youville Clinic Web site: http://www.youville.ca/english/news.html or the Heart and Stroke Foundation Web site: http://ww1.heartandstroke.mb.ca/Page. asp?PageID=28&CategoryID=16.

The manual contains all the recipes and lessons, as well the nutrition activity master sheets for photocopying. It also provides contact information for organizations where other nutrition education materials in the kit can be ordered. Kit contents are listed at the end of this summary.

Any community group or organization wishing to teach kids about healthy eating and food safety can use this kit without any training. This project was an opportunity to pool scarce financial and human resources to create a unique tool that can be used by communities. Kids in the Kitchen was a collaborative project between the Winnipeg Regional Health Authority, Manitoba Milk Producers, First Nations and Inuit Health Branch (Health Canada), Youville Clinic Inc., and The Heart and Stroke Foundation of Manitoba.

Food security includes food skills. Kids in the Kitchen makes food safe, healthy and fun.

For more information contact:

Joyce Slater or Pat Bugera-Krawchuk
184 Chestnut Street
Manitoba Milk Producers
Winnipeg, Manitoba
P.O. Box 724
R3G 1R6
Winnipeg, Manitoba
(204) 774-5563
R3C 2K3
jslater@mts.net
(204) 488-6455

patbk@milk.mb.ca

Kids in the Kitchen Community Action Kit Contents:

Sturdy plastic carrying tub with lid
'Kids in the Kitchen' manual
Canada's Food Guide to Healthy Eating & Northern Food Guide tear sheets
Food safety package (decals, brochures, magnets)
1 Hackey Sack ('Bean Bag Toss' activity)
1 Bandana/Blindfold ('Psychic Powers' & 'That Makes Scents' activities)
12 Aprons
1 Food Guide felt rainbow ('Food Rainbow' activity)
6 Measuring cup sets
6 Measuring spoon sets
1 Plastic sleeve ('Who am I' activity)
Spices ('That Makes Scents' activity)
Fight BAC video ('Fight BAC Video' activity)
Fight BAC Game ('Fight BAC Game')
BAC Catcher ('BAC Catcher Game')
Food safety questions and answers ('BAC Catcher Game')
Nutrition bingo ('Nutrition Bingo' activity)
Food model cards ('Favourite Breakfasts' & 'What Am I?' activities)

For additional copies of print resources, ordering information can be found on pages 140 & 141 of the manual.

Queensway Community Garden

Ed and Lynn were supportive of the idea, and a community garden planning committee was formed with representatives from the Native Friendship Centre, Porter Community House, Community Gardens Prince George Society, and Make Children First. The group submitted a proposal through the Aboriginal Subcommittee to Make Children First for grant monies to cover the purchase of three sets of gardening tools, a storage shed and a push-reel mower, and expenses associated with two Community Days to promote and celebrate the garden. Funding was approved and the garden came to life in the summer of 2003.

The location of the community garden is heavily supported by research. The Early Development Instrument, implemented in Prince George in 2002, indicates that the kindergarten children in the VLA and South Fort George areas of the city are vulnerable in terms of their physical health and well-being. Food access maps completed by the Make Children First Nutrition Educator show that the cost of adequate nutritious foods for a family of four for one week could consume up to 25% of a family's weekly income in these same areas of the city. Finally, the Child Health Profile of Prince George (2002) identified that the number of children living in poverty in the city is above the national average, which hampers access to nutritious foods.

An Agency-Based
Gardening Initiative
by Danielle Sykes

The Queensway Community Garden is a unique project managed by a group of service providers and concerned citizens who came together to develop a vision for, and then create, a multi-agency and public community garden in the VLA/South Fort George area of Prince George. After two years, the garden has found eight agency partners, and several other local groups rent plots for program use.

Background

The idea for a community garden for use by service organizations to benefit their clients was generated by Emma Faulkner, Coordinator of the Emergency Food Resources Program at the Native Friendship Centre, Jovanka Djordjevich, Coordinator for the Community Gardens Prince George Society, and Danielle Sykes, Nutrition Educator with the Make Children First Initiative of Prince George. Ms Faulkner approached Ed and Lynn Gilliard, residents of Queensway Avenue, who were willing to explore community usage of a one-acre parcel of their land to benefit residents of Prince George. Their land had been used in the past by emergency food providers to grow food for hampers.

Vision

The community garden partners envisage a community garden that includes plots for agencies to run client based programs and to grow food for agency services (i.e., for a hamper program or agency community kitchen), as well as public plots to be rented for the growing season. The Queensway Garden strives to:

• Empower people, and empower communities to empower people

• Increase community capacity to work together to ensure access to healthy and affordable food

- Provide skill-building opportunities through organized client work parties and public educational workshops

- Enhance local emergency food services through a principle of "hand-up" instead of "hand-out" (i.e, agencies providing skill-building for clients, helping clients build community relationships, and obtaining emergency food for hampers, etc, through participation and cooperation)

- Bridge social, economic, cultural and environmental boundaries

- Create a safe, and cooperative environment by being:
- Inclusive and culturally sensitive
- Supportive
- Community-driven

Roles and Responsibilities of Garden Partners

The role for the Queensway Garden Partner is to work toward the realization of the above vision. Garden Partners will work collaboratively with others to fulfill the administrative responsibilities of making the community garden run. These responsibilities include organizing clients/ public plot renters and assigning duties or plots; obtaining Garden Member Agreement Documents from all participants; and fulfilling other miscellaneous administrative tasks, depending on agency policy or program parameters.

Garden Partners are responsible for signing the commitment agreement to ensure that they provide:

- regular and consistent staff representation at all administrative member meetings (eight to ten per year), work party days, and community days

- staff to manage administrative duties for client participation or programs, and some financial or in-kind support (e.g., tools, supplies, garden maintenance)

The commitment agreements are reviewed and renewed annually.

2003 Season Highlights

Despite the late start, due to the timing of funding, the garden partners planted, grew and harvested respectable amounts of produce. Garden participants were mostly staff people, and the nature of the agency/client relationship of the garden partners lent itself more to one-time garden experiences rather than consistent client programming. However, all partners expressed great successes as a result of being involved and participant surveys revealed that those who had participated learned new skills, took home fresh vegetables and experienced greater mental health.

Completed projects for 2003 included laying a garden path, the construction of a tool shed, and a composter-building workshop.

The 2003 season concluded with a Community Harvest Day to showcase the project and harvest the produce. The public was invited to the garden to see the success of the project, and to enjoy a free, catered lunch created with vegetables from the garden. The event was a great success, with many people interested in being involved for 2004. Porter Neighborhood House reported the following:

This was an event that helped to create awareness for the Porter Community House and the services we provide. In October we held a harvest party where all the participants in our garden plot cleared the garden of the remainder of the produce. We shared all the produce with the growers and left many bags of assorted vegetables in the carport of the Porter Community for access by area residents.

Pat Ellis, Porter Community House Garden Representative

The Native Friendship Centre expressed its success:

… over 240 people visited the garden, including many clients who usually visit the soup bus to supplement their families' weekend meals. While there, children, youth, adults and Elders pulled potatoes out of the ground, picked carrots and peas, ate chili prepared with vegetables out of the garden, and connected with one another. It was a wonderful opportunity for clients dependent on emergency foods to participate in a healthy, positive and respectful event that introduced them to connection with the land, life cycles and growing foods.

Emma Faulkner, Emergency Food Resources Coordinator, Native Friendship Centre

The garden planning committee gained valuable insight from the partnership with the Community Gardens Prince George Society. The success of that group's public community garden space, and the expertise of that garden's coordinator, helped to shape the administrative guidelines and manage the day-to-day maintenance requirements of the Queensway Garden project.

2004 Season Highlights

The 2004 garden season brought several new partners, including Northern Health Community Mental Health programs, the Prince George Metis Elders' Society, the Prince George Dakelh Elders' Society, and the Prince George chapter of the Salvation Army. All Garden Partners from 2003 returned for another season – no small success in itself! With the support of Community Gardens Prince George Society, the Queensway Garden planned and built 16 public plots, which were rented to the public and to two groups – a family visiting program, Families Count, and a church group, Riverside Community Church.

One of the noted successes of 2004 was the complete integration of the garden into program planning for Northern Health Community Mental Health (NHCMH). Seven of eight support groups participated at the garden, with Mental Health staff, life-skills workers and clients working side by side as frequently as twice per week. NHCMH is now considering revising

job descriptions to include gardening tasks in association with this project, and other Garden Partners are investigating ways to incorporate the garden more fully into client programming. This approach allows clients who are still dependent on stage-one food-security programs to gradually move to stage-two food-security initiatives with the support of trusted individuals in a safe and protected environment.

The participation of a second emergency food resource, the Salvation Army, is another great success of 2004. While finding volunteers to help with the garden was often a challenge, the Salvation Army harvested several hundred pounds of potatoes to distribute through its hamper program. This agency's partnership resulted in fresh, local produce for hamper recipients, and also encouraged the participation of several half way houses to maintain the plot, promoting skill-building for these volunteers and allowing them to "give back" to the community in a meaningful way.

Projects in 2004 were many and varied. In response to participant surveys from 2003, the Queensway Garden partnered with a local environmental organization to host a summer employee to work on the largest project, a Northern Varieties Demonstration Fruiting Garden. While the project is far from complete, many valuable steps were taken and the project will continue to grow over the next several years. The garden also garnered the support of the City of Prince George, which is enthusiastic about partnering in 2005.

The Queensway Garden was also host to the Healthy Eating Active Living (HEAL) Northern Routes Caravan tour in June as a best practices showcase of a healthy eating, active-living initiative in action. For the event, the Queensway Garden offered a greenhouse-building demonstration, organic green tasting with local homemade dressings and a number of children's activities. The greenhouse is durable, simple in design and materials can be purchased for less than $150 – a great backyard project to extend the short northern growing season.

The season closed again with a Community Harvest Celebration, and another spread of dishes created with garden produce for the public and garden members to sample. Garden Partners reported harvesting, combined, more than 1500 lbs of potatoes alone! Other vegetables grown and harvested included cabbages, broccoli, brussel sprouts, zucchini, pumpkin, and much more.

The Queensway Garden enjoyed many more successes and certainly had its share of challenges. Transportation for client groups and garden security posed the greatest challenges, as well as volunteer involvement and the maintenance of communal areas. However, the successes experienced and shared by all groups far outweighed the challenges. One Garden Partner shared:

The garden has given [our] clients something to look forward to next season. [it has given them] hope.

NHCMH Staff, Group Success Report

Looking Forward to 2005

The third season at the Queensway Garden will be one of growth and opportunity. With the involvement and support of the City of Prince George, seeds will be started in late winter for the Queensway Garden, and plans are being made to hold a workshop on starting seeds, pruning seedlings and transplanting young plants.

Other projects for this year include the development of the Demonstration Fruiting Garden, a message board for garden members, a pergola for gardeners and garden meetings, workshops and the development of integrated preschool curriculum to increase the use of the garden by preschool-aged children.

The Queensway Community Garden is community development at work. Its potential for increasing food security in our city is obvious, and its blending of stage-one and stage-two food-security actions is unique and exciting. It is a privilege to be involved in such a groundbreaking project.

The Participatory Food Security Projects

*of AHPRC & Nova Scotia
Nutrition Council*
by Christine Johnson

Since their beginning in 2001, the Participatory Food Security Projects have evolved tremendously and have included a continuous series of interrelated projects. The projects have been a partnership between the Atlantic Health Promotion Research Centre, Nova Scotia Nutrition Council, and staff and participants of Family Resource Centres/Projects throughout Nova Scotia, and have been both provincial and national in scope. The projects have done much to increase the profile of the issue and build capacity among individuals, communities, organizations, and systems to address root causes of food insecurity. The Food Security Projects have been based on several key questions.

Question 1: How much does a basic nutritious diet cost in Nova Scotia?

In 1988, a study was done to answer a simple question: How much does it cost to purchase a basic nutritious diet in Nova Scotia? The answer was clear. People living on a low income could not afford to eat nutritiously. In 2000 it was recognized that more recent information was needed. But more than just updating the figures, the partners also wanted to build capacity in

communities for food costing activities as well as to find a way to keep the information current by having the question answered regularly.

To help build capacity, a participatory research approach was taken. Staff and participants of Family Resource centres were engaged in a "train the trainer" model to do "food costing" research in each region of the province. The overall outcome was not only to re-establish that a nutritious diet is not affordable for many Nova Scotians, but that this model of participatory food costing served as a point of engagement to participatory processes and a catalyst to community mobilization, as well as enhanced capacity of professionals and their respective organizations and those affected by food insecurity to work together to influence policy.

To help find an ongoing role for food costing, the Office of Health Promotion for the Government of Nova Scotia (OHP) agreed to support further research to a) develop a model for the ongoing monitoring of the cost of a healthy diet, and b) to explore policy options for building food security in Nova Scotia. This research will build on the past involvement of OHP in the Food Security Projects.

Question 2: What is life like for people who don't have enough nutritious food?

Many of the people who worked on the food-costing project knew from personal experience, even before the food-costing results were in, that the cost of a nutritious diet is too high for many to afford. The project partners thought that capturing stories of people's experiences dealing with food insecurity was important The stories would also allow all Nova Scotians the chance to better understand the struggles and hardships individuals dealing with food insecurity face in their everyday lives and, along with the food costing data, could be powerful in advocating for policy changes that would build food security.

To do this, "story sharing workshops" were held throughout the province, using a similar "train the trainer" approach as with the food costing. The workshops allowed for the identification of the problems related to food security, what causes the problems, why these problems are important to address, and what could be done to address them.

Question 3: What is being done to deal with food insecurity and to build long-term solutions?

Many of the food security issues that were identified in the food-costing and story-sharing pieces of this research point to both problems and solutions in government policy. This highlighted the need to find ways of dealing with the immediate impact of food insecurity on people's lives as well as looking for long-term solutions. Looking at existing policy as well as potential policy changes to make sure that public policy actually improves food security can lead the way to effective, long-term solutions. The project partners thought the best way to answer this question was to ask people working on food security across Canada to share their experiences and strategies in trying to influence policy. More detailed information was found by talking directly to some of these people. The findings of this work told how they tried to influence policy, what worked, what didn't, what challenges they faced and what they learned. As well, they shared some tips for influencing policy.

Question 4: What more can we do to improve food security and take action?

The people who have been working on the food security projects in Nova Scotia want to do something with the findings. They want to make a difference in their communities and influence policy that will make all Nova Scotians more food-secure. The national partners also want to use this information in their own areas and to try to make a difference at a national level.

The projects were able to support communities in bringing people together to have dialogues to discuss the issue and the findings of the research in their areas.

In addition to this, two major ways identified by the research to address food security in communities was to first build a common understanding of the issue of food security and then to provide information and tools so help people to take action to have an impact on policy. S, to further facilitate dialogue on food security and policy within communities, not only in Nova Scotia but nationally, the project partners developed a resource titled "Thought About Food? A Workbook on Food Security and Policy. This workbook is available on-line at www.foodthoughtful.ca . A workshop process was developed and used to pilot the workbook provincially and nationally, to test its effectiveness in meeting its desired goals and objectives to broaden the understanding of the issue and to try to affect policies that play a role in food security.

After this pilot is completed and the workbook finalized, CAPC and CPNP projects across the country will be brought into a process of training on the implementation of the "Thought about Food?" workbook to enhance knowledge within CAPC/CPNP projects related to food security and policy through training in the use of the workbook and to build capacity within CAPC/CPNP projects related to their role in building a foundation for policy change. Also, a video will be produced to help build awareness of food insecurity, its underlying causes and strategies for addressing it, highlighting the use of the "Thought About Food?" workbook.

In addition all this work, two National Dialogues were held throughout the projects. These dialogues strengthened the network of people working on food security across the country, increased awareness about the Nova Scotia Food Security Projects, and engaged participants in discussions on food-security and policy-related issues. Dialogues also brought people together to identify current national food-security issues and to give input into the tools and process developed in Nova Scotia.

Learnings

The Participatory Food Security Projects have occurred as a result of the continued commitment of our provincial and national partners and their dedication to participatory approaches to build food security. In particular, it was found that organizational structures that enable participation were key to engaging communities in this work.

Further to this, the participatory processes used were instrumental in building commitment and buy-in for the projects. These processes do, however, take time and project activities and outcomes must remain flexible to accommodate the diverse contexts, capacities and needs of the many partners involved. Adequate monetary support is also required to support the participation of community members.

Overall, the Participatory Food Security projects have laid the foundation for community action on policy through capacity building for food costing and community-generated evidence to support policy change.

For more information on the Food Security Projects and copies of our reports, please visit www.nsnc.ca.

Cooking Fun for Families

by Dawne Milligan

Cooking Fun for Families (CFF) is a school-based nutrition education and health promotion program for inner-city families. It was developed in Vancouver, BC, in 1996, and now operates in ten to twelve inner-city elementary schools in Vancouver. It was developed to complement school lunch programs with a focus on improving families' long-term nutritional status and food security. The main goals of the programs are (1) for participants to acquire food- and nutrition-related knowledge and skills through learning and active participation and to apply these at home with their families, when possible, and (2) for participants to enjoy the program, get to know other participants and enhance their social networks and social support.

Most of the CFF programs take place in the inner-city schools, either in specially designated parents' areas, or in the staff room or lunchroom. Occasionally, they take place in a nearby community centre. There are one or two staff at each program. Some staff are neighbourhood workers already present at the schools, while others are hired as outside staff. Funding for food supplies and for the outside staff has been secured from a number of sources, including the municipal health department, charit ableorganizations,business organizations, religious organizations and individuals.

Programs consist of meal planning and cooking and eating together, and vary from about two to six hours. They take place once a week and each involve from 4-15 or more parents. Two of the programs include children in food preparation. At six programs, parents, or parents and their children, eat a meal together at the end of the session. Several programs give participants leftover food to take home for their families to try.

Preliminary evaluation of the CFF program in 1996 found several perceived benefits, relating to (a) increased food preparation skills, knowledge and awareness of nutrition and healthy eating, (b) parents' increased feelings of trust and comfort level with the school, (c) parents' enjoyment of participating in a program together with their children, and (d) enjoyment of preparing and eating a meal together. Some of these benefits are reflected in the following quotations taken from interviews with participating parents:

My kid is demanding different food now. I couldn't believe this guy! I could not believe this guy would eat raw vegetables! For a couple of years I've been trying to get him to eat vegetables, and he always hated them. Now he eats raw vegetables. He says he likes them! It's amazing! That's been a very good effect for him. [Single father]

My youngest one, now, when we're making something, she'll know, she knows what nutrition is and what's good for you. And she'll tell me there has to be vegetables with the meal. She's right into the nutrition things now. If it's not nutritious, she won't eat it. [Single father]

A manual was prepared detailing how the program was developed and how to create a similar program. It includes steps such as: preplanning and building support for the program, assessing your community's readiness to start the program, identifying your goals and objective; developing your strategies; deciding how the program will be administered; preparing a budget and applying for funding; and how to evaluate your program.

The manual is available on the Vancouver Community Kitchens Website at: www.communitykitchens.ca/cookingfun.htm.

From 2001-2004 a more formal valuation of Cooking Fun for Families was undertaken by a research team of academic and community partners in Vancouver, BC, funded by the Social Sciences and Humanities Research Council. Results of the evaluation will be submitted for publication soon. The evaluation research produced a 14-minute video of the program, which may be purchased by contacting one of the people below.

Barbara Crocker
Community Nutritionist
Vancouver
Coastal Health
1292 Hornby Street
Vancouver, BC
V6Z 1W2
(604) 714-3400
barbara.crocker@vch.ca

Diane Collis
Vancouver Community Kitchen Project
1150 Raymur Avenue
Vancouver BC
V6A 3T2

tel: 604-876-0659 ext 118
fax: 604-876-7323

cooking@uniserve.com
www.communitykitchens.ca

Project LINK for Health

Local Investment in Nutrition Knowledge
by Sarah Robert

Project LINK for Health started when one teacher at one school voiced her concern about the nutritional quality of the food her students were eating. Three years later, Holy Family Catholic Regional Division No. 37 has adopted a division-wide Nutrition Policy; has a registered dietitian on staff to coordinate the health initiatives; provides an annual School Division Nutrition Calendar to all families in the division; offers healthy cooking classes; and is actively working to address health issues in all the division schools. Funded by the Public Health Agency of Canada's Population Health Fund, Project LINK for Health strives to empower students, staff and families to build healthy lifestyles, despite challenges such as budget concerns and lack of time.

The Nutrition Policy was written with input from students, parents, teachers and school board members. This process, although time consuming, is necessary to ensure that the policy meets the needs of all the stakeholders. Presentations by dietitians about some of the health issues facing today's students helped to build support for the policy. An implementation guide was developed for each of the schools to address some of the common concerns such as fundraising, classroom rewards and where to find helpful resources.

The policy also used a phased in-approach – requiring the schools to have vending machines, canteens and cafeterias with 50% of choices from the "Choose and Serve Most Often" and "Sometimes" lists by the end of the 2003/2004 school year, and 100% by the end of the 2004/2005 school year. Again, by drawing out the timelines for implementation, schools have been able to adjust successfully.

For the past two years, a School Division Nutrition Calendar has also been a very popular component of our project. This calendar features photos of students from each of our schools, with recipes, health information and tips. The calendar is mailed out to all the families in our division free of charge. Feedback has been phenomenal – families appreciate the healthy recipes and reminders about the importance of healthy living all year long.

Cooking classes are offered at each of our schools and taught by a registered dietitian. These classes have a focus on healthy, low-cost, quick recipes and all recipes use common household ingredients. Discussions during the classes cover label reading, shopping on a budget and meal planning. Students enjoy the classes and, even months after a class, are often observed eating the food they learned to make at school.

Having a health project throughout the whole school division can be challenging because schools are geographically separate and each community is unique. Monthly health themes have allowed us to have consistency across the division, to address a variety of different health issues, while still encouraging each school to take ownership of health-promotion activities for their own communities. Each school sends a staff representative to a monthly Communication Seminar. At the seminar, statistics and background information are provided about the theme, and the group discusses how the theme relates to their students and school communities, ideas on how to engage their school communities and various stakeholder groups, and how to deal with time and financial limitations.

Often discussions cover using health-promotion activities to meet the curricula for various subjects and grade levels.

These seminars have been very valuable in providing a network of support to persons involved in health promotion. This is essential to building and maintaining motivation and direction! After the seminars, the representatives return to their schools and work together with students, parents, and/or other staff members to plan and implement an activity related to the monthly theme.

Many of the schools in our division have designated a bulletin board in the school to feature the monthly health theme. Staff members, parents, and students from a wide range of grade levels have all been involved in designing and creating bulletin boards. A fact sheet on each theme and an update on project activities are sent home to all the families in the division with the monthly school newsletters. School activities have been creative and exciting. For the theme of "Lunching and Munching," one school did a school-wide "Chicken Soup for the Soul Luncheon," celebrating healthy food choices and involving students and family members in organizing the event, preparing the food and carrying out the event. For the theme of "Hug Your Heart for Heart Month," one high school is having students write facts about heart health (related to risk factors, prevention of heart disease, and human physiology) on heart-shaped paper. The hearts will be stuck to walls and ceilings throughout the school and be connected by veins and arteries all leading to the heart of the school – the cafeteria.

Division-wide initiatives are also planned several times a year in which schools compete against one another. The Movin' and Groovin' Across Canada Challenge had all the schools in the division keeping logs of time spent being active. Each school's progress across the map was tracked on our Web site (www.hfcrd.ab.ca) and schools reported increases in both school spirit and activity levels. Emphasis was placed on active living rather

than organized sports in order to include everyone. Students from all schools in the division and ranging from ECS to Grade 12 participated. Activities ranged from sports such as volleyball or football to raking leaves and chasing chickens! Other division-wide initiatives included "Happy, Healthy Holiday BINGO" to help maintain healthy lifestyles over the Christmas holidays, and "Celebrate the Rainbow of Healthy Eating Day," in which students dressed up as their favourite fruit or vegetable and had a recipe exchange. Tame the TV Week is planned for April 2005.

Project LINK for Health has been a huge learning experience for everyone involved. Various school staff have reported that previously they did not realize the impact of healthy eating and active living on students' performance and behaviour at school. Now, through involvement with Project LINK, schools are actively promoting health and students, parents and staff members are all involved in supporting each other in their quests for health. School division administration has recognized the need for health promotion and the benefit of a comprehensive school health approach, and so Project LINK for Health will continue after funding ends and further explore partnerships with other departments within the school division. We have learned the importance of stakeholder involvement and ownership of the project. We have seen challenges and successes, and have chosen to learn from both. The schools in Holy Family Catholic Regional Division No. 37 continue to build capacity for health promotion. Community development is happening in our school communities and everyone is sharing, learning, growing, and benefiting because of it.

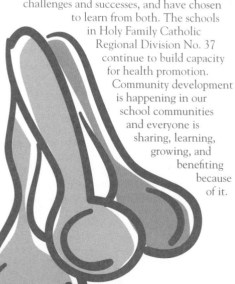

Gleaning Program

Access to Fresh Fruit And Vegetables at No Cost! A Food Security Initiative Supported By York Region Food Network
by Karen Aagaard and Fae Chen

Packed into a yellow school bus, balancing boxes and baskets on their knees, gleaners gather with children intow. The bus lurches forward as the driver shifts the vehicle into gear, barrelling down Davis Drive in Newmarket, Ontario. Each passenger will soon see traffic lights and noisy cars replaced by strawberry bushes and muddy boots. In a matter of minutes – 20 or so empty baskets will be full of fresh, farm-picked strawberries.

The Gleaning Program was established by Fresh Food Partners, a task group consisting of partners from York Region Health Services, York Region Food Network, and community agencies and members in 1999. This innovative program enables families living in York Region, primarily those living on a limited income, to pick or "glean" their own fresh produce at no cost. At the end of the harvesting season, local York Region farmers invite these families to pick fruits and vegetables that would otherwise go to waste or be ploughed under.

As a result, gleaning participants are able to enjoy excellent quality strawberries, apples, corn, peppers, zucchini, squash, tomatoes, broccoli, cauliflower and cabbage.

Gleaning participants bring their children along to help out in the field. This provides a great opportunity for children to learn where their food comes from.

All participants have the desire to provide their families with fresh and nutritious produce, produce they otherwise could not afford. What appears, at first glance, to be a simple program is a little more complex when all pieces of the program puzzle are pulled apart.

There are essentially three pieces of the puzzle: the providers (the local farmers and their families), the task group (those who organize, implement, and fund the program) and the gleaners (those who participate in produce-picking). It is only when all three puzzle pieces link up with each other that the Gleaning Program can take place. In 2004 Fresh Food Partners hosted nine gleaning trips. Over 215 individuals participated and they gleaned over $5000 of fresh produce.

After an hour of gleaning, once again gleaners are back on the yellow school bus. This time, the empty baskets are filled with luscious strawberries. Their sweet smell filters through the air. Conversation is taking place and recipes are being exchanged. As the final destination is reached, gleaners are tired but excited, and looking forward the next trip.

Meal Bags

Ready-to-Cook
Ingredients & Recipe
by Maureen Perlmutter and Gail Wylie

A Meal Bag contains the recipe for a nutritious meal that will feed four to eight people and the non-perishable and measured ingredients, needed to make it. Meal Bags are available to women who attend Healthy Start drop-in programs for $1.50, a cost representing from 50-100% of the total cost of production. Any perishable ingredients needed must be purchased by the family, but these are always minimal, simple and inexpensive. Meal Bags can help stretch the family's food budget and create a skill-building opportunity.

Meal Bags were actually devised with another idea in mind – for streamlining the demands of producing meals at multiple locations each week. The idea of making them available to participants came as a second, sudden, positive thought, inspired by the Good Food Box model in Toronto. Charging a nominal sum fit with our belief that the charity model needs adapting, that women should be offered choices and that paying creates pride.

In addition to cost and nutrition, Healthy Start for Mom & Me Meal Bags are designed with several other considerations in mind.

For example:

• All Healthy Start for Mom & Me Meal Bag recipes can be made using minimum kitchen gear, some needing only a pot, a spoon and one burner. (Most women who attend our drop-ins have simple kitchens with only basic equipment, tools and utensils.)

• All Meal Bag recipes require only basic cooking techniques, typically mixing, stirring and using an oven or burner. In addition, recipes are written clearly, in plain language, in numbered steps that can be followed easily. (Some participants have little or no cooking experience; literacy may also be an issue.)

• Meal Bag recipe ingredients are commonplace, linking participants to foods that are easy to find. (Some participants have little experience with healthy food shopping, or with food shopping in Canada. In addition, getting around is a significant challenge: most women who attend our drop-ins have to food shop within walking distance of their homes and are therefore restricted to a limited number of food stores.)

• Meal Bags can be kept on hand safely for several months and saved for a "rainy day". (Most participants are low on money near the end of the month. Those who have our Meal Bags may be somewhat less reliant on food banks and other sources of emergency aid.)

• Meal Bag recipes can be readily adapted to suit the family's cultural food traditions, individual tastes and religious requirements. Newcomers to Canada feel they are learning to cook "western" or "Canadian" foods.

Families buy Healthy Start for Mom & Me Meal Bags for many reasons: to supplement their food budget; to try out new foods at minimum cost; to introduce new foods to family members at minimum cost; as emergency food; to "kick start" a healthy eating plan; to practise cooking.

Staff dietitians adapt or develop the Meal Bag recipes. Soups are frequent and we occasionally do desserts. Recipes are often field-tested with participants or with a small group of moms whom we pay to cook, taste and revise to ensure the Meal Bags are as useful and tasty as they can be. Recipes include such things as: Tomato Bean Soup, Rice & Chick Pea Salad, Chicken & Vegetable Fettuccini (canned chicken), Taco Soup, Spaghetti with Tomato-Lentil Sauce, Peach Crumble.

For the labour-intensive job of assembling Meal Bags (we make up to 2000 at a time), community volunteers are involved, such as classes of middle school students. This gives a good opportunity to engage community members in our work and for discussion of food security and other poverty issues. Bulk buying enables the project to be cost-effective.

At Healthy Start for Mom & Me, Meal Bags serve a dual purpose of creating a skill-building, food-security option for participants as well as a time-saving way of managing simple cooking in a large program. The Meal Bag concept has been adopted by some other groups and in particular by the First Nations and Inuit Health Branch's Canada Prenatal Nutrition Programs in Manitoba which produced a "how-to" manual. Others may find the concept useful too–community kitchens, food banks, cooking classes, community cupboards or food-buying clubs.

Healthy Start for Mom & Me has been running drop-in outreach programs since 1997 in low-income Winnipeg neighbourhoods. We work with pregnant women and girls, and those with infants up to one year, who, in the face of considerable social and economic barriers, are striving to improve their chances of having healthy, successful pregnancies, and their newborns' chances of optimal development. They are especially interested in information, skills, strategies and tools that help them meet their own and their families' nutritional needs. Healthy Start is funded by the federal government's Canada Prenatal Nutrition Program and by the provincial government's Healthy Child Manitoba. For the initial start-up and development years, Healthy Start was sponsored by Dietitians of Canada. Healthy Start for Mom & Me is now an incorporated organization with its own Board. Healthy Start works in collaboration with many other local organizations and includes involvement from public health nurses.

Food Services at the University of Winnipeg

by Kerniel Aasland

During the winter of 2002, the University of Winnipeg Students' Association (UWSA) began a lengthy process aimed at running food services at the U of W campus. This culminated in the spring of 2004, when the UWSA submitted a bid in competition with many other multinational corporations. Although the UWSA bid made the short list, it did not ultimately win the contract. Despite this, the more than two years spent developing the bid were useful and informative and created a number of other tangible benefits.

There were many reasons why a food services bid was pursued. The food services were, and still are, contracted out to a multinational company. This, in turn–meant that the food is treated as a tool to make money - and its quality suffered. This also meant that the profits from the food services left the campus and the community. The UWSA wanted to change all this: the UWSA wanted to improve the quality and variety of food on campus; it wanted to reinvest the profits back into the campus and community; it wanted to run the food services in a way that better served the larger community, with an eye towards community and local economic development. To meet these goals, several different processes were used throughout the planning and bid creation.

It is one thing to want to increase the quality and variety of food on campus; it is quite another to deliver food that is healthy and what people want. So one of the early steps for the UWSA was to do a large survey with students. Just under 200 surveys were collected and the results were used as a guide in determining what kinds of food should be offered at the different locations around campus, and what types of activities people wanted to see in conjunction with food services.

In connection with this, lots of time was invested in exploring all the different educational, employment, economic and community opportunities that could be found within food service. The food services are primarily a daytime operation, meaning that the kitchens could be available for other purposes in the evenings, at night, on weekends and during much of the summer, and many different ideas flowed from this thought:

• The facilities could be used to host a community kitchen in the off-hours.

• They could be rented out in the off-hours–at cost–to community-based micro-enterprises who needed access to a kitchen in order to meet food safety and health codes so that they could then sell their products to local restaurants.

• They could be used to host cooking classes for students and community residents, and there were many groups that expressed interest in this.

One of the realizations that came from the survey results was that students were interested in a broad array of foods. So, the planning worked to address this in two ways. The first was to deliver significant portions of the menu in a "pay by weight" buffet format. This meant that food would be prepared in smaller batches, or dishes, to be placed in the buffet and a broad range of items could be offered in this way. Secondly, partnerships were formed with a number of exciting community restaurants that offered unique and specialty cuisines.

Each of these restaurants was invited to bring their specialties on to campus for a week at a time. Students gain by having access to specialized variety. Food services gains by not having to learn 30-plus cooking styles in order to deliver this variety. Local restaurateurs gain sales and exposure on campus. Most restaurateurs also agreed to offer a cooking class as well. It was a win-win proposition for everyone involved.

Another aspect of the UWSA food service plan was to take steps to differentiate each food service outlet from each other. The largest would host the majority of buffet-style "pay by weight" offering along with traditional cafeteria food. The second largest would host the offerings from local restaurants and offer specialty pizzas along with a limited "traditional cafeteria menu." The coffee shop would be expanded into a coffee house, with a small performance area. Over lunch hours and in the evenings, this would be used to host a variety of art and spoken-word shows along with book launches, research presentations and local musicians. All this would be geared to making this facility the social and cultural hub of the campus.

A number of environmental initiatives were also proposed, such as the introduction of commercial composting, developing a waste-reduction plan, shifting away from disposable items where practical, introducing bulk condiment dispensers alongside the individual packets and offering a coffee discount for people who brought their own mugs.

On the community development front, many different ideas were brought forward, as well. The composting site would link into the existing network of community gardens as end users of the compost. A U of W community garden would also be established, and all the gardens could be become suppliers to food services. Many of the specialty grocery stores in the community are not only locally owned and operated, but they offer many products difficult to find elsewhere. Using these local suppliers also has a greater economic multiplier effect in the local communities around U of W.

Wherever possible, the UWSA tested out the feasibility of these ideas. We met with community organizations, food banks, residents' associations and local restaurant managers, and visited specialty grocery stores. Many of the plans and ideas had to be changed as a result of these meetings, and the many partnerships formed the basis for other new and exciting ideas to emerge. A town hall was held on campus to present the different ideas and plans, along with samples from the menu, and was very well received. Along with all this, the UWSA was also busy raising the capital necessary to launch and run the new food service. A complex corporate structure was also created that would allow for direct university, community and student input into the operations of the food service, and interim directors were found.

The bid was finalized and all the research, thinking, planning, money, corporate structure and hopes of the participants found their way into the proposal. The UWSA bid was good enough to make the short list, and we were invited to make a formal presentation. The final contract was not awarded to the UWSA food services bid, but many of the ideas and initiatives are nonetheless being implemented. U of W now houses a community gardening project and is investigating commercial-style composting. More attention is being paid to waste reduction issues, and the menu, although not stellar, continues to be expanded. The relationships built with local community organizations are also valuable, and will foster many new and exciting initiatives in the future.

The Development of Arctic Co-operatives Limited The Development of Arctic Co-operatives Limited
by Andre Goussaert

The harsh climate and the environment of the Arctic Barren Land were a never-relenting hindrance for the Inuit to find food. The Inuit philosophy concentrated completely on the idea of "nutrition" to sustain life. Life in the Arctic imposed upon its people a culture of survival. Surviving on the Arctic tundra and its coasts was a merciless struggle; harvesting food and the region's treasures was always a challenge: unpredictable and never secure. How was it possible for the Inuit to survive for hundreds of years? Working together was an inherent and domineering principle that saved generations of Inuit in the small nomadic groups spread over the vast Arctic region. It could be seen in the hunting patterns and survival techniques and in the consensus building throughout the social fabric of their society.

The Canadian government accepted responsibility for the Arctic region in 1880 but, for the longest time, paid very little attention to this region. Several factors triggered its attention towards the North in the fifties: the cold war and the fear of Russian invasion; the public outcry over stories of abject poverty, starvation and disease; the stir

among southern entrepreneurs to tap into the northern mineral wealth; and the drive to include all Canadians in a uniform, national social safety net.

The cold war and the fear of Russian invasion in the fifties directed attention towards the defence of the northern border of the North American continent. The American military machine got the okay from the Canadian government to set up the DEW Line right across the Arctic about 200 miles above the polar circle–a station every 50 miles. It was a tremendous undertaking and many stories could illustrate the impact on the Inuit population. It also left a stark image in the minds of the thousands of workers who worked on the building and the maintenance of the DEW Line.

Secondly, a public outcry started building over stories of abject poverty, starvation and diseases. Farley Mowatt's book *People of the Deer,* telling the story of starvation and misery, caused quite a concern within government circles. I remember vividly my own experience dating back to 1958 when many people starved to death in the Back River area before our help could reach them. The subsequent message to all government administrators was to be on guard and never let people starve to death, regardless of the cost.

There was also an impatient stir among southern entrepreneurs to tap into the northern mineral wealth, which was gradually being brought to light by the many surveyors who had been criss-crossing the Arctic at the peril of their lives for many years. The Arctic was hiding a multitude of riches waiting to be excavated and to create wealth.

Finally, there was the drive to include all Canadians in a uniform, national social safety net. Child support and old age pensions were brought in for the Inuit population in the fifties. As there were no birth records in many cases, guesses had to be made about the age of people and who qualified for the old age pension.

Medical facilities were gradually being provided to northern and remote communities.

All these pressures were driving government actions in the North and reshaped the Arctic societies sometimes in a brutal way. Amid all this, the formal co-operative movement was initiated and grew.

Since the early fifties government officials started discussing cooperatives as a possible vehicle for social and economic development of the northern peoples, and in 1958 the federal government announced its first five-year, northern cooperative development program and a year later, the co-operatives in Port Burwell and George River were incorporated as small production co-ops.

These promising starts encouraged people in other communities and by the mid-seventies there were 41, of which 30 were in the former Northwest Territories (NWT). In many places government officials and missionaries worked along with the people to reach a better understanding in the operation of the cooperatives. Most started as small production co-ops with very few resources. Starting businesses differed from community to community. In some, the co-ops' first commercial ventures started with the production, buying and selling of art, and in others, it was a commercial fishery or the provision of municipal services.

In general, these first operations were seen as stepping-stones towards "more and better." In some places, artists agreed to take very little money for their art in order to build up capital, start a retail store and provide themselves with more variety of imported foods. Already, in the sixties, a few people had ventured in the retailing food business, be it on a small scale. Transport was one of the major factors driving up the capital outlay to get into the retail business in the North, as most of the communities were supplied once a year during the short summer season. All food inventories had to be bought once a year, requiring a once-a-year large outlay of capital, and no fresh produce or dairy were available.

This was the way the Hudson's Bay Company (HBC) operated its trading posts. A few basic food items such as flour, powdered milk, sugar and pilot bread were available in their stores, with a year's supply of these items stored away in their local warehouse.

Koomiut Co-operative in Pelly Bay had to find a solution to the transport problem, as there was never a HBC store in Pelly Bay. People had to travel hundreds of miles by dog team to neighbouring communities to buy some most-needed merchandise. In the late sixties, the co-op built its own runway and started operating its own DC4 freighter plane, which brought in merchandise and a better selection of food on a regular basis.

Effective cooperative movements usually organize in federations, groupings or alliances to achieve benefits of scale by working together to purchase jointly whatever goods or services they need, to collaborate in training programs, to sell collectively and to lobby government when needed. Discussions about forming a federation of cooperatives began almost at the same time as the northern movement itself.

In 1966 an important meeting with delegates from all northern coops took place in Povungnitok (northern Quebec) and a decision was made to form federations of co-ops to provide them with much-needed services such as management assistance, education, consolidated buying and marketing. The Quebec legislation already permitted the formation of such institutions and the Northern Quebec Federation of Co-ops was incorporated in 1967. However, nothing existed yet in the NWT, as 1967 was the year the administration of the NWT moved from Ottawa to Yellowknife, and co-ops were not the first item on the agenda. It was another five years before it became a possibility. The northern government was pressured by the co-op membership, so finally, the federal government took the initiative to facilitate the incorporation of a federation for the NWT coops.

In 1972 delegates from all the existing coops gathered in Churchill, Manitoba and after a few days of intense negotiation 26 cooperatives signed the incorporation documents. One strong motivator for signing the incorporation documents was the possibility offered by Koomiut Co-operative to benefit from the plane operation. In order to do so, all goods in transport had to belong to the federation. The plane operation had already shown its contribution towards improving food security.

Regular flights into the Arctic ensured a continuous availability of a larger selection of nutritious food, such as fruit, vegetables and dairy. In one instance, the freighter took a load of 350 cases of apples from the Okanagan across the Arctic to several co-operatives. The change in prices, to quote only one instance: the freighter DC4 brought goods to the Repulse Bay Co-operative at 18.5 cents a pound, versus 75 cents prior to the operation of a co-op federation-owned and-operated plane.

In the first years of operations there were multiple growing pains but, through it all, the big picture was never abandoned and there was no turning back. The Federation of Arctic Co-operatives became a shining example of community-based economic development.

Co-operatives got involved in a large variety of businesses. The retail businesses of food were outgrowing all the other ventures, in volume. Management and employees competence kept improving. We should not underestimate the complexities of conducting business across such a vast region: distances, difficult and expensive transportation, high cost of northern construction and challenges in creating effective and uniform accounting systems. The remoteness of the communities demanded the development of an effective transportation infrastructure and Arctic Co-ops, over the years, built a logistical system that includes a wide range of delivery methods – truck, aircraft, barge, ship and the federal government's Food Mail program, which makes healthy foods available in northern communities at reduced rates.

The operations of the co-ops provided more and more jobs giving the people more assurance and security.

In most communities, the co-op installed and ran cable TV operations and their federation Arctic Co-ops got into a partnership in ARDICOM to help introduce a high-speed digital communication network to the North.

The North is very exposed to the broader world now and people in the communities want the same food products on the shelves at their co-op store as the ones they would see in our big cities. Ensuring that fresh products and staple commodities make it to the co-op shelves is a complex operation. For the most remote communities, Arctic Coops' re-supply program stocks up 50% of co-op inventories once a year. Products shipped by sea (about 80,000 cubic metres) are coordinated in Montreal and transported north by Nunavut Sealink and Supply, a joint-venture company directed by Arctic Co-ops. It takes careful planning to order for a whole year and to manage the inventory over a 12-month period.

From its small beginnings the cooperative movement in the North has grown into a multi-million-dollar operation: revenue of the co-ops last year were $124 million, employing 800 people in the local communities, all of which is owned by 18,000 community members.

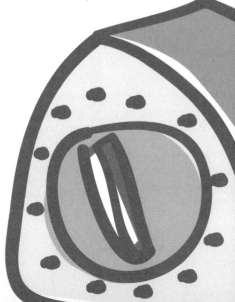

Foodlink Waterloo Region

A Community Approach to a Healthier Food System in Southern Ontario
by Peter Katona with Marc Xuereb and Ellen Desjardins

Building a Rural-Urban Consensus

In the summer of 2000, a small group of individuals, including representatives of Region of Waterloo Public Health, the Food Bank of Waterloo Region and the Community Garden Network of Waterloo Region, got together to discuss ways to strengthen Waterloo Region's food system. Although our community already had several food-security initiatives underway, it was decided that they might be improved by a more coordinated and structured approach, linking the different aspects of a community food-systems agenda. Public Health started the process by determining interest and priorities and soliciting ideas as to what might be done. It funded and carried out a number of preliminary consultations and a forum with community stakeholders, including farmers and farming organizations. It was clear that there was interest in creating a new independent organization, called Foodlink. Stakeholders felt that the organization should not be urban-dominated, but should have strong representation from farmers and rural interests.

Three basic roles were envisaged:

• To lead collaborative research projects on various aspects of the local food system (especially food security issues including food access and distribution).

• To develop and promote a "food localism" movement highlighting direct connections between producers and consumers.

• To initiate and access funding for existing and potential grassroots projects addressing food systems themes.

With the continued guidance of the Public Health department, a steering committee was formed by local food-security and food-systems advocates to incorporate Foodlink Waterloo Region as a not-for-profit organization. With incorporation and the subsequent establishment of a functioning board of directors (including rural and urban constituents), Foodlink began to tackle various components of its food-systems mandate through the development of three separate working groups, facilitated by Region of Waterloo Public Health staff. the Buy Local working group explored "food localism" initiatives, The Food Boxes working group looked at "food accessibility" issues, and the Urban Agriculture working group promoted community gardening, working in collaboration with the existing network of community gardens.

Of the three, the Buy Local working group met with the greatest success, guiding Foodlink to the creation of its "flagship" project, the Buy Local! Buy Fresh! map–a directory of 30 farm-gate sales listings in Waterloo Region. The map, produced in partnership with Public Health, was funded by the Agricultural Adaptation Council's Canadapt program and 40,000 copies were printed and distributed in 2002.

Organizing the Rural-Urban Connection

In December of 2002, Regional Council agreed to provide initial financial support for Foodlink. A one-time start-up grant of $50,000 enabled Foodlink to hire its first full-time staff and establish an office.

112

Foodlink again partnered with Public Health to produce a second Buy Local! Buy Fresh! map in 2003. It also facilitated the establishment of two new initiatives; a weekly electronic bulletin, Foodlink Fridays, and a Foodlink Web site. Both the Web site (which also received funding from the Toronto Community Foundation) and Foodlink Fridays were intended as information clearing houses for food-systems work regionally and elsewhere.

With the hire of the first coordinator in June 2003, Foodlink began to look at its own development as an autonomous institution. Topping the agenda was the need to develop new funding partnerships and revenue streams. Other major priorities included drawing new stakeholders into the "food localism" movement, and maximizing impact through service delivery. The Foodlink board undertook a strategic planning process to add form and clarity to its work. It was decided at this time that Foodlink would concentrate on "food localism," and leave "food security" to others.

A mission statement was developed, reflecting Foodlink's core values:

Foodlink Waterloo Region promotes a healthy food system that sustains both food producers and consumers in our community. By linking rural and urban concerns, we will create an awareness of the true value of local food, and foster initiatives that make its production more viable and accessible throughout the Region.

With broader food systems in mind, Foodlink further refined its organizational mandate to guide existing and future programs and initiatives, as follows:

Together with farmers, consumers and community stakeholders, Foodlink seeks to:

1. Promote healthy, local food

2. Add value to local agricultural production

3. Improve consumer access to local food by supporting new markets

Tangible Support for a Broad Mission

With a mission and vision in place, the Foodlink Board of Directors examined its projects and services and developed a series of linked activities that focussed on marketing support for local food producers and consumer education on the availability and importance of local food products. While work began on a third edition of the Buy Local! Buy Fresh! map, Foodlink launched a new monthly publication, named Local Harvest, which replaced Foodlink Fridays. Local Harvest was designed to "tell the story of local food," profiling a seasonal food product (including its history, varieties, storage tips, production and health benefits) along with profiles of local farms listed on the Buy Local! Buy Fresh! map. Distributed electronically to Foodlink Friday's 120 subscribers, Local Harvest, with its unique combination of consumer education and hands-on marketing assistance for local producers, was well received. In its first year, readership grew to over 650 direct e-mail recipients. Local Harvest is also shared via several other list-serves and its posting on the Foodlink Web site has encouraged more visits to the Foodlink site.

With the publication of the 2004 Buy Local! Buy Fresh! map, community interest in Foodlink and food localism gained considerable momentum. The number of farms on the map increased from 39 to 76 (with each paying $50 to list), and the map continued to receive much media attention. Included on the list were some "downstream" urban retail outlets – to make locally grown products more easily accessible for readers. Another subtle addition involved having farms identify which products they themselves grew or raised –often country markets and roadside stands will make purchases to augment their own production. This distinction, along with a "seasonal availability guide," was intended as an additional step that provided consumers with information as to what products are truly local. The 2004 map also featured paid advertising spots on the map in hopes of increasing revenues to sustain the initiative. The Region of Waterloo continued to provide financial and in-kind support for the publication.

Foodlink and Public Health agree that the long-term viability of the Buy Local! Buy Fresh! map will hinge on sustainable revenue, and as such are reviewing farm-listing fees and increasing efforts to attract advertising for the 2005 edition.

Along with the Buy Local! Buy Fresh! map, Foodlink was also expanding its support for other local marketing initiatives. In July 04, the Old Order Mennonite community established a wholesale produce auction, which served as a twice-weekly sales venue for more than 100 farms in the area. Similar produce auctions are gaining popularity throughout the United States and this was the first of its kind in Canada. At the request of EPAC, Foodlink helped with marketing materials, lined up buyers and produced price reports for the first year's sales. Considered a consistent outlet for higher value crops, the produce auction has the potential to expand local supply for a variety of customers, including restaurants, small retail, country markets and farmers' market vendors. EPAC held 23 auctions between July 20th and October 15th. While individual product prices varied at each auction, overall sales grew considerably and the EPAC management was sufficiently pleased the results. Foodlink will continue to promote this new enterprise, as it has great potential to localize the supply and consumption of seasonal fruit and vegetables.

In September 2004, Foodlink convened its first Taste Local! Taste Fresh! event in partnership with the Perth, Waterloo, Wellington Chapter of Canadian Organic Growers (COG). With funding received from ACE Bakery (via the Toronto Community Foundation), Foodlink and COG hosted 350 people at an afternoon event showcasing local food. Fifteen farms from the Buy Local! Buy Fresh! map were paired with chefs from 15 local restaurants. Each pairing created a specialty dish featuring a farm-fresh product and guests had the opportunity to meet both the chef and farmer while sampling an array of creative appetizers.

Each guest also received a "passport," which provided information about the host organizations and their causes, the farms and restaurants and the actual recipes of the dishes they tasted.

The event received outstanding media coverage and was attended by a good cross-section of the community, mixing regional politicians and local agriculture organization representatives with urban activists, food enthusiasts and consumers. Along with boosting the profile of food localism and the host organizations, a very positive outcome was the establishment of direct business contacts between the restaurants and farms.

Into the Future

In October of 2004, Foodlink was able to procure substantial funding from the Ontario Trillium Foundation. The two-year grant primarily covers core operations and funding for contract staff, and will allow Foodlink to continue refining its community niche and services. Foodlink is expected to prepare a business/marketing plan to guide its work into the future. Perhaps one of the largest challenges facing Foodlink is to arrive at an appropriate balance between community food-systems education and the provision of marketing services to farms and food-related enterprises. New partnerships are being explored in the community to strengthen and sustain existing activities as well as create new opportunities to market and consume more local food. The MBA program of Wilfrid Laurier University has been commissioned to assist Foodlink's board, advisory committee and staff in developing marketing and awareness programs that move beyond "farm-direct" sales. Some potential areas that Foodlink may pursue include local food labelling and the development of a "regional brand," an electronic marketplace, retail and restaurant recognition programs and the creation and promotion of local wholesalers/distributors.

Please visit http://www.foodlink-waterlooregion.ca/ to learn more.

Eating from the Salad Bar

*Healthy Food that
Children Want to Eat*
by Debbie Field

Farm to School Salad Bar in California

In November 2001 I was invited to Los Angeles to give the keynote address to a conference on food issues, A Taste of Justice. In the months before the conference, I had been reading e-mails from the US about a new way of delivering school lunch programs and I was very keen to get a first-hand look at the Salad Bar Program to see if the reality was as exciting as the e-mail version. I asked the conference hosts if I could tour the Farmer's Market Salad Bar program in Santa Monica, one of the school districts of LA.

On Friday, November 2, I borrowed a car and followed precise instructions through the LA traffic maze to McKinley Elementary School, which had launched the first Farmers' Market Fresh Fruit and Salad Bar four years earlier on September 17, 1997.

I was given a tour by the nutritionist hired by the Santa Monica-Malibu Unified School District to support the salad bar programs in its 14 schools. As we entered the cafeteria, there were two small rooms where food was being served. If you turned to the one on the left, a staff member served a traditional United States Department of Agriculture (USDA)-funded hot lunch. If you turned right, you entered the salad bar area.

On the day I visited, the USDA lunch program was serving deep-fried chicken balls, two slices of white bread, two thin celery sticks, a tiny paper cup of cheese dip dressing, a larger paper cup of canned pineapple slices and a small pint of USDA Surplus milk. About 150 of the school's 500 kids had chosen that lunch the day I was there.

In contrast to Canada–where there is no national policy framework or history of promoting school-based meal programs–the USDA program has its roots in the Great Depression of the 1930s when the Roosevelt government launched three interconnected, programs to address urban hunger and farm price crisis. Standing in a wheat field in Iowa in 1933, the Secretary of Agriculture, Henry Wallace, declared a "new deal" for farmers who had to burn their wheat because they could not get an adequate price, and for the millions of people in the cities who couldn't afford bread.

The government of Franklin Delanor Roosevelt set up three United States Department of Agriculture (USDA) surplus food programs. The first bought food from farmers at stable prices and warehoused it for future need. The second provided low-income people with food stamps, allowing them to get free food through established retail food outlets. And the third was a nationwide, universal, hot lunch program in which all school children had access to a free or subsidized hot lunch, often made up in large part from USDA surplus agricultural products. Based on a means test, children from low-income families received these meals for free or at a reduced rate.

In recent years, USDA lunch programs have been criticized for creating as many social problems as they solved. Jan Poppendieck points out in *Sweet Charity: Emergency Food and the End of Entitlement* (New York: Penguin Putnam Book, 1999) that the USDA policies stigmatized low-income families and children in particular because they rest on a means test: you have to prove you are poor to qualify. And rather than help the small farmers who most needed it, the Roosevelt program tended to provide the richest farmers with the largest subsidy because they had the largest tracks of farmland. In fact, the current global fight against US farm subsidies traces its roots to the policies developed under FDR.

Because there was only limited attention paid to the type and quality of food served in subsidized hot lunch programs or available through food stamps, these programs did not necessarily promote the healthiest foods. Recent studies of the lunches served throughout the US have shown them to be too high in fat, salt and sugar, and lacking in fresh fruits and vegetables. In fact, some researchers have pointed the finger at school lunch programs, along with fast food lunches, as one of the factors driving the childhood obesity crisis in the US.

Nevertheless, standing in the well-equipped cafeteria in LA that day, I was grateful for many decades of funding for student nutrition programs in the US. When I was growing up in NYC, my family was poor enough to qualify for the program and I received a free hot lunch every day. I remember the mashed potatoes, frozen peas, meatloaf and gravy, all of which are comfort foods for me to this day. My mother, who was a widow and working full-time, describes how the hot lunch program took the pressure off her because she knew that I had at least one healthy meal at school and she could prepare a simpler meal for my dinner.

The subsidized hot lunch program didn't change my mother's low-income status, but it did reduce the impact of our poverty and contributed to my health and well-being. (It probably also laid the basis for my lifelong interest in food and student nutrition programs, an interest that I have pursed in my years at FoodShare!) But I also remember the stigma of lining up with my girlfriend and going our separate ways when the line divided between the poor kids in the hot lunch line and the better-off kids who brought their packed lunch from home and ate in the regular cafeteria. It's no small irony that I was almost certainly getting the better nutritional deal even as I learned a painful lesson about social inequality.

Increased sensitivity to the relatively poor quality of food served in the USDA hot lunch programs, and, to a lesser extent, the stigma of targeting programs for poor kids, prompted Robert (Bob) Gottlieb to develop the Salad Bar program alternative to the traditional hot lunch. Bob is the founder of the Americium Community Food Security Coalition and his children attended primary school in the Santa Monica-Malibu Unified School District. He was teaching at Occidental College and was able to recruit student volunteers to do the preliminary research on setting up the salad bar program, and connecting it to the expanding farmers markets in LA.

The Salad Bar program was founded and sustained by colleagues in the US who share the vision and analysis of groups like FoodShare in Canada. Our mission is: "Working with Communities to Improve Access to Affordable Healthy Food – From Field to Table." For over a decade we have worked with our partners in the Boards of Education, the City of Toronto's Board of Health and other community groups in designing and implementing student nutrition programs from the ground up, school by school, and eventually throughout the whole City of Toronto.

In LA, the salad bar program was organized by the Center for Food & Justice (CFJ), a division of the Urban & Environmental Policy Institute at Occidental College (UEPI).

What groups like FoodShare and the Center for Food & Justice have in common is our commitment to healthy food rather than just any food. Both groups strive to improve the nutritional quality of food served in student nutrition programs. We believe that children deserve the very best food in our society – not fast food or surplus food that may jeopardize their health. Both groups are also concerned with sustaining small farmers and building the market for local and organic farm products among urban consumers. We promote field-to-table or direct farm-to-school programs to accomplish these goals.

Getting back to that day in November at McKinley Elementary, my other choice was to turn right and sample the salad bar lunch program being served up. It consisted of eight, cut-up, vegetable options, eight cut-up, fruit options, four cut-up protein options (including tuna fish, egg salad, ham and peanut butter), and four carbohydrate options (several kinds of breads and crackers). The day I visited, about twice as many children chose the salad bar option. When they piled up nothing but cherry tomatoes and grapes, the staff member encouraged them to take some protein, just as they had been "taught in your classroom."

The remaining 50 primary school students had packed their own lunch, and most of them had pop, chips and a mixture of mass market "lunchables." It was quite a stark reminder that the better-off kids face many of the same nutritional challenges as poorer kids and can even end up eating worse food. Parents, under pressure to combine convenience with appeal, end up concocting elaborate junk food meals, filled with name brand chips, pop and the various specialized lunch snacks that continue to line the supermarket aisles.

The Santa Monica student nutrition programs benefit from the infrastructure and financial support of the USDA. They have funding to purchase equipment and hire staff. In Canada we do not have any federal support for school-based nutrition programs. This is one of the few social policy issues in which the US is ahead of Canada. In the absence of a federal program, Canadian communities must struggle on a city-by-city or school-by-school basis to raise funds to make healthy meals available to children during their school day. This has to change.

The California school I visited had an automated financial system whereby children swiped an electronic card as they left the serving area, paying either the full rate of two dollars per lunch or a subsidized rate for low-income families. This was a solution that was virtually stigma-free. A big improvement since my school days in New York!

I admit I'm biased but it seemed to me that the children eating from the salad bar were eating more of their food than anyone else was eating. There also seemed to be less waste in terms of packaging or thrown-out food. The kids who brought their own lunch from home were discarding mountains of elaborate packaging.

There are salad bar programs all over the United States. The Santa Monica programs are particularly exciting because they are integrated into a farmer's market approach where as much of the vegetables and fruits as possible is purchased from the local farmer's market. Every attempt is made to make sure that the items chosen for the salad bar are culturally appropriate to the students who are eating it. And unlike most of our student nutrition programs in Canada, because of the support of the Santa Monica-Malibu Unified School District, the program is integrated into a more comprehensive educational approach. The nutritionist who gave me the tour is allocated the time to go into the classrooms of the 14 schools in the district, teaching kids how to choose properly when they eat at the salad bar, and also teaching them about agriculture and food policy.

The Santa Monica-Malibu Unified School District Farmers' Market Fresh Fruit and Salad Bar is also part of the Farm to School program. Through this educational and classroom approach, children learn about farming and farmers, visiting farms or having farmers and chefs come into their classroom. Composting and community gardens are also encouraged at each school. This enables the school board to go beyond the salad bar as a feeding program, to the salad bar's becoming integrated into the curriculum and a holistic approach of educating school aged children about nutrition, food and agriculture.

I was tremendously moved by what I learned in LA that day, and wanted to see if we could start a similar program in Toronto.

The Canadian Feed the Children – FoodShare Partnership

While I had been learning about US salad bar programs, Halima Aman, a staff member of Canadian Feed the Children was also learning about them. She had begun discussions with parents and educators at Winchester Public School here in Toronto to see if they wanted to add the salad bar and a community garden to their already successful healthy lunch program. Halima and others at Canadian Feed the Children provided the funding that enabled FoodShare to pilot two salad bar programs in the spring of 2002. Since that time we have continued to work with local schools and there are now over 15 schools that have tried the salad bar approach and are implementing it at least a few days a week at their school.

I think the most incredible part of the salad bar pilots has been the children's enthusiasm to eat a healthy lunch. Even those of us who most strongly believe that children will like healthy foods eventually have been pleasantly shocked at the way the kids gobbled up the healthy salad bar lunch, almost from the moment it was presented to them.

Here in Toronto, after 15 years of work, we have the most developed network of school-based nutrition programs in Canada. Over 75,000 children eat a healthy breakfast, lunch or snack in one of more than 400 programs operating at over 350 community and school sites. Each program manages itself, involving local parents and school members to make it culturally appropriate to the children who are being served. And, through the Toronto Partners for Student Nutrition, a partnership of all the Boards of Education, the Department of Public Health and community agencies like FoodShare, there are funding and support to help programs get organized and become sustainable. In 2004-2005 we received $2.5 million of city funding, and over $1 million of provincial funding to help programs.

So, when a new idea like the salad bar comes along, there is some infrastructure and capacity to make it happen.

With childhood obesity on the rise, and the continued and increasing disconnect between food production on farms and urban life, the Farm to School and Salad Bar approach seems so sensible. It is a practical way for parents, schools and kids to learn about healthy eating in a positive and fun way. Imagine the power of reaching children at school with a positive message about healthy eating and adding gardens and composting to school breakfast, lunch and snack programs for an integrated and holistic approach to food. It is so simple and elegant but so important.

The Emergence of Food Security in B.C Public Health

by Barbara Seed and Dr. Aleck Ostry

Community Nutritionists in British Columbia are excited about the imminent possibilities for food security in BC Public Health. We are on the cusp of a new era!

Food security has been approved as a Core Program in the newly released "BC Public Health Core Programs," and food- security programs and policies are beginning to be enhanced at the Regional Health Authority (RHA) and community levels.

This case study provides a superb example of the importance of collecting evidence and creating readiness for an opportune time to further the food-security agenda in the BC government. There's quite a story to tell of how front-line staff, health professional associations and civil society have propelled us toward this juncture in BC, and I hope to capture some of the highlights.

Many factors have led to the increased interest in food security by the BC Ministry of Health Services (MOH). Interest was piqued in the early 1990s when the then Provincial Nutritionist, Anne Carrow, came back from a conference to meet with the BC Community Nutritionists and waxed eloquently about the future vision she saw for food security. Concurrently, interest and

awareness were also building through the efforts of Laura Kalina, Community Nutritionist, who was completing work on her book *Building Food Security in Canada*, as Sydney Massey of the BC Dairy Foundation led the development of the first *BC Food Guide* and as Farm Folk City Folk was founded in Vancouver.

Interest coalesced in 1997, when the BC Heart Health Coalition, Food Security and Nutrition Advocacy Committee published a report entitled *Feed Our Future, Secure Our Health*. This report used a population health approach, focussing on food access, food supply, nutrition behaviour and skills and nutrition services. It called upon the provincial government to develop a Provincial Food Policy. The BC MOH responded in The Provincial Response to *Feed Our Future, Secure Our Health* (1998) by highlighting inter-ministerial efforts to address food and nutrition issues, and, in 1999, established an inter-ministerial working group to explore coordinated approaches to food and nutrition policy. This group included representation from the BC Heart Health Coalition and was jointly chaired by the MOH and Ministry of Agriculture and Food. At the time, however, other economic, social and health issues took precedence, and the policy environment did not appear ready for inter-sectoral collaboration at the provincial level. However, MOH representatives brought information from this group forward to the Select Standing Committee on Agriculture and Fisheries in 2000, highlighting best practice in coordinated approaches to food policy, which, due to this effort and that of many others, was reflected in the first report of the Select Standing Committee.

A joint initiative between the Community Nutritionists Council (CNC) of BC and Dietitians of Canada, BC Region, provided a further contribution. The *Cost of Eating in BC* report has been published annually since 2000. It concludes that British Columbians living on a low income, especially those families on income assistance, cannot afford to access safe and healthy food in a dignified manner.

The authors of the report have met with various provincial Ministers and senior staff to advocate for those living on a low income.

In the fall of 2002, a new opportunity presented itself. Dr. Trevor Hancock had been hired by the Ministry of Health to draft the new Public Health Core Programs in BC. We were thrilled, as Dr. Hancock had a great reputation in health promotion, and was instrumental in the establishment of the Toronto Food Policy Council. He encouraged us to submit an evidence paper to make the case for the inclusion of food security in core programs. To this end, the CNC Food Security Standing Committee secured funding from Health Canada and later received additional funding and support from the BC Government Employees Union and the Interior, Vancouver Coastal, Vancouver Island and Northern Health Authorities.

The goals of the resultant paper, *Making the Connection–Food Security and Public Health* were to:

• Provide evidence that lack of community food security is a critical public health concern

• Provide evidence that community food-security interventions are effective in promoting health and preventing food-related illness and disease, and

• Identify the role of the health sector in building community food security in BC

The report was published in 2004, and is now available on the BC Public Health Association Web site at: www.phabc.org/pubs.html. Blood, sweat and tears went into this paper; it took almost two years, three writers and many, many editors to complete!

Making the Connection–Food Security and Public Health made the following recommendations:

• Ministry of Health designate food - security as a core public-health function

• Health Authorities include food-security strategies as part of their Health Services

Redesign Plans and provide resources for implementation

• Health Authorities incorporate food-security strategies as part of their health information database and planning and monitoring processes

• Health Authorities participate in the development of regional food-security (or policy) councils and champion the development of a provincial food policy council

Another situation was brewing concurrently that would also support our efforts. In the fall of 2003, we had a historic meeting with the BC Medical Health Officer's Council (HOC). At this meeting, a resolution for a Public Health Alliance on Food Security between the HOC and the CNC was passed. This joint meeting had been spurred on through presentations given to the HOC earlier that year, which included a persuasive talk on the *Cost of Eating in BC* report. The Public Health Alliance on Food Security now also includes representation from the Environmental Health Officer's Council and the Public Health Nursing Leadership Council. It also has links to the BC Public Health Association, the BC Food Systems Network and the BC Provincial Health Service Authority.

Another key provincial MOH strategy will facilitate further integration of food security into BC Public Health. The BC MOH has initiated Act Now! BC, designed to improve the health of individuals and communities by focussing on five goals for BC's population by 2010. One of the goals relates to Healthy Eating, with the objective of increasing by 20% BC's population who eat recommended daily servings of fruit and vegetables. A number of healthy eating initiatives are included in the program. Most directly related to food security is a Community Food Action Initiative, a grant program to support projects like community kitchens and gardens and "Good Food Boxes"; the MOH will be working with the BC Public Health Alliance on Food Security,

RHAs, and other ministries to develop a plan for implementation in 2005/06. Also, a School Fruit and Vegetable Program providing one serving of BC. grown fruits or vegetables two times a week to children at ten elementary schools will be piloted around the province. This program is a collaborative effort between the MOH and the Ministry of Agriculture, Fisheries and Food.

The impact of civil society in the process cannot be understated. Public awareness regarding food issues such as hunger, health and obesity, food safety issues, loss of farmland and environmental impacts of non-sustainable farming practices has increased.

This, combined with targeted funding for food security initiatives, has contributed to an escalation of activity at the community and grassroots levels; it is burgeoning in the form of food-policy councils, food charters, networks, innovative programming and research. While it is a discredit not to mention the many successful and influential grassroots organizations and networks, it is also difficult to mention some and not others. These groups are successful not only in their own right, but also in providing the groundswell to influence government action. The annual "Sorrento Gathering," hosted by BC Food Systems Network, has facilitated the growth of this groundswell by providing a place for those from diverse places of interest to gather and learn from each other and develop a plan for coordinated action. With the increase in public recognition of food as related to health, the issue can begin to be framed in a broader way – that is, one of food security.

While the opportunities for food security as a "Core Public Health Program" are great, key challenges also lie ahead. Food security has a long way to becoming a "mature" public health program – embedded at both the provincial and RHA levels. Champions need to be identified at both the senior level of the MOH and at the RHA levels.

RHAs are at differing stages of incorporating food security into their business plans. Food Security Consultants have been hired in three of the five RHAs. It is hoped that the Act Now! BC food-security initiative and the adoption of Core Programs will facilitate the hiring of Food Security officers in the final two RHAs. To further the integration of food security at the RHA level, the CNC contracted a paper to be written on food-security indicators. The CNC views this indicator document as a first step toward the development of a more comprehensive set of indicators, and encourages people to test the indicators in their work; it was a challenge to create indicators that reflected a comprehensive concept of food security, yet were narrow enough to fall within the jurisdiction of a health authority and the framework of public health. This is a challenge that will persist as Public Health assumes a leadership role in community food-security. While public health initiatives may be required to define or report its food security work in narrow way, community-based initiatives should not then be "medicalized," "individualized" or otherwise dictated by Public Health objectives and indicators. Specifically, policy, advocacy and system redesign objectives are more difficult to measure than individualized programs, so will be a challenge to incorporate into a public health model of food security.

At both the government and RHA levels, it will be a challenge to frame the concept of food security in a way that will be understood and accepted across disciplines and ministries; there are competing interests and priorities. Whether at the level of the MOH, the RHA or the Public Health Alliance, we need to move forward with great care, with a particular emphasis building trust in our newly formed partnerships.

Wish us luck, good sense and a lot of patience!

Editor
Anna Maria Kirbyson

Editorial Committee
Herb Barbolet
Mustafa Koc
Jean Charles LeVallee
Chris McCarville
Todd Scarth

The Food Project
Executive Committee
Carol Ellerbeck
Paul Fieldhouse
Larry McLennan
Terri Proulx

Contacts/Contributors

Section One:
Social Justice and
Hunger Alleviation

Nigel Baseley
West Broadway Development Corporation
640 Broadway
Winnipeg MB
R3C 0X3
204-774-6851

Chokey Tsering
Canadian Association of Food
Banks (CAFB)
www.cafb-acba.ca
www.think-food.com
416-203-9241

Nathalie Dupuis
Coordonnatrice
Regroupement des Magasins-Partage
de l'île de Montréal
514-383-2460

Marie-Noëlle DeVito,
Chargée de projets,
Moisson Montréal inc.
6880, chemin de la Côte-de-Liesse
Montréal PQ
H4T 2A1
514-344-4494
Télécopieur: 514 344-1833
info@moissonmontreal.org
www.moissonmontreal.org

Gerry Pearson
Healthy Living Coordinator
St. Matthews-Maryland
Community Ministry
Winnipeg MB
204.783.6159
Fax: 204.774.1847
diabetesprevention@yahoo.ca

Connie H. Nelson, PhD
School of Social Work
Lakehead University
955 Oliver Road
Thunder Bay ON
P7B 5E1
807-343-8447 or
807-767-0480
cnelson@lakeheadu.ca

Charles Z. Levkoe
Urban Agriculture Coordinator
The Stop Community Food Centre
P.O. Box 69, Station E,
Toronto ON
M6H 4E1
416-652-7867 ext. 236
Fax: 416-652-2294
charles@thestop.org
www.thestop.org

Basha Rahn
Advocate Child Poverty Action
Committee and the Social Planning
Advisory Network of Williams Lake,
Williams Lake BC
250-243-2380
brahn@wlake.com
and
Tatjana Bates
Community Nutritionist,
Interior Health Authority, BC
250-398-4622
tatjana.bates@interiorhealth.ca

Karen Schlichting
PR and Events Coordinator
LITE (Local Investment
Toward Employment)
509 Selkirk Ave.
Winnipeg MB
R2W 2M6
204-942-8578

Section One:
Social Justice and
Hunger Alleviation

Maureen Barchyn, PHEc
Staff Development Coordinator/Clinical
Supervisor Family Support Program
401-393 Portage Avenue
Winnipeg MB
R3B 3H6
204-947-1401
Fax: 204947-2128
mmbarchyn@familycentre.mb.ca
www.familycentre.mb.ca

Wayne Roberts
Policy Coordinator
Toronto Food Policy Council
277 Victoria Street, Suite 203
Toronto ON
M5B 1W1
416-338-7937
Fax:416-392-1357
tfpc@toronto.ca

Steve Andrews
Youth Service Coordinator
Collingwood Neighbourhood House
5288 Joyce St.
Vancouver BC
V5R 6C9
604 412 3844
Fax: 612-412-3844

Kay Yee
Nutritionist
Regina Qu'Appelle Health Region
306 766 7651
wkyee@sasktel.net

Section Two:
Sustainable Food Systems

Cathleen Kneen
S-6, C-27, R.R. #1
Sorrento BC
V0E 2W0
phone/fax: 250-675-4866

Lisa Kell
Malaspina University - College,
Bachelor of Science in Nursing
Fourth–Year Student
3980 Telegraph Rd
Cobble Hill BC
V0R 1L0
250-743-9254
Lallylocks@shaw.ca
and
Mark Timmermans
Providence Farm
1843 Tzouhalem Rd
Duncan BC
V9L 5L6
250-746-4204
www.providence.bc.ca

Sunday Harrison
Green Thumbs/Growing Kids
care of Toronto Kiwanis Boys
and Girls Club
101 Spruce St.
Toronto ON
M5A 2J3
E-mail: sunday@interlog.com
Phone: 416-876-1480
www.kidsgrowing.com
(currently under construction)

David M. Neufeld
Agriculture Committee of the
Turtle Mountain Community
Development Corporation
Personal contact: 204-534-2303
Box 478,
Boissevain MB
R0K 0E0
www.roomtogrow.info
roomtogrow@mts.net
TMCDC contact: 204- 534-6303
or 1-800-497-2393 or
turtlemountain@mts.net,
Box 368,
Boissevain MB
R0K 0E0

Sharon Taylor
204-779-8546
staylox@hotmail.com

**Jessi Dobyns, Karine Rogers,
Karen Sutherland**
Seasoned Spoon
1600 West Bank Drive
Peterborough ON
K9J 7B8
705-748-1011 ext 1290
seasonedspoon@yahoo.ca
www.trentu.ca/opirg/seasonedspoon

Jane Rabinowicz
Rooftop Garden
Project Coordinator
Santropol Roulant
4050 rue St. Urbain
Montreal QC
H2W 1V3
514-284-9335
Fax: 514-284-5662
www.santropolroulant.org

Will Braun
Wiens Shared Farm collective
Farm contact info:
Wiens Shared Farm
1208 PR 200
St. Germain South, MB R5A 1H3
204-255-7027
wilmadanwiens@mts.net

Don Kossick
111 Albert Ave.
Saskatoon SK
S7N 1E6
306-665-6185 or 306-220-3584.
saskfoodsec@sasktel.net
kossickd@sasktel.net

Jane Hayes
Learning Grounds Project Manager
Evergreen
355 Adelaide Street West, Suite 5
Toronto ON
M5V 1S2
416-596-1495 x. 227
Toll free: 1-888 -426-3138
Fax: 416-596-1443
www.evergreen.ca

Wendy Mendes
PhD Candidate ~ Food
System Policy & Planning
Department of Geography
Simon Fraser University
Vancouver BC
wendy_mendes@sfu.ca

J. Tom Webb
Program Manager
Master of Management Co-operatives
and Credit Unions
St. Mary's:
902-496-8170
tom.webb@smu.ca
Antigonish:
902-863-0678
jtwebb@auracom.com

Mustafa Koc, PhD
Associate Professor
Department of Sociology
Ryerson University
350 Victoria Street
Toronto ON
M5B 2K3
416-979 5000 ext. 6210
Fax: 416 979 5273

Karen Lind and
Dr. Stephane McLachlan
Environmental Conservation Lab
211 Isbister Building
Department of Environment and
Geography, University of Manitoba
Winnipeg MB
R3T 2N2
204-474-7949
Fax: 204-474-7699
umlindkm@cc.umanitoba.ca

Jessica Thornton
30 Brunswick Avenue
Toronto ON
M5S 2L7
jmthornt@hotmail.com
647-880-8567

Susan Roberts, RD
Project Coordinator,
Growing Food Security in Alberta
163 Street,
Edmonton AB
T5R 2P2
780-484-9045.
Fax: 780-484-9099
susanr@cbr-aimhigh.com
www.foodsecurityalberta.ca

Sarah Robert, RD
Project L.I.N.K. for Health
Holy Family Catholic Schools
10307 99 Street
Peace River AB
T8S 1R5
780-624-3956
Fax: 780-624-1154

Christine Johnson, MSc., P.Dt.
Project Coordinator, Food Costing
Atlantic Health Promotion
Research Centre
Suite 209 City Centre Atlantic,
1535 Dresden Row,
Halifax NS
B3J 3T1
902- 494-6038
Fax: 902-494-3594
christine.johnson@dal.ca

Andre Goussaert
209 Brock Street
Winnipeg MB
204-489-7269
agoussaert@shaw.ca

Kristin Hildahl, RD
Staff Development Instructor
WRHA Home Care Program
1-189 Evanson Street
Winnipeg MB
R3G 0N9
204-940-2459
Fax: 204-940-2009
kjhildahl@wrha.mb.ca
www.wrha.mb.ca

Gail Wylie
Manager
Healthy Start for Mom & Me
400 Edmonton St., 2nd floor,
Winnipeg MB
R3B 2M2
204 -949-5354
Fax: 204-949-4800

Elizabeth Brims
Executive Director
York Region Food Network
194 Eagle Street
Newmarket ON
L3Y 1J6
905-967-0428
yrfn@bellnet.ca
www.yrfn.ca

Danielle Sykes, BSc
Nutrition Educator,
Make Children First Initiative
Northern Interior Health Unit
1444 Edmonton Street
Prince George BC
V2M 6W5
250-649-7072
Danielle.Sykes@northernhealth.ca
www.makechildrenfirstpg.org

Barbara Crocker
Community NutritionistVancouver
Coastal Health
1292 Hornby Street
Vancouver BC
V6Z 1W2
604-714-3400
barbara.croker@vch.ca
and
Diane Collis
Vancouver Community Kitchen Project
1150 Raymur Avenue
Vancouver BC
V6A 3T2
604-876-0659 ext 118
Fax: 604-876-7323
cooking@uniserve.com
www.communitykitchens.ca

Shefali Raja, BSc, RD
Community Nutritionist
Vancouver Coastal Health
Evergreen Community Health Centre
3425 Crowley Drive
Vancouver BC
V5R 6G3

Barbara Seed, MPH, RD
PhD Student
Community Nutritionist
BC Community Nutritionists' Council
c/o Fraser Health Authority
Public Health Nutrition Program
Berkeley Pavilion
15476 Vine Ave
White Rock BC
V4B 2C8
604-542-4002
Fax: 604-542-4009
barbara.seed@fraserhealth.ca
and
Dr. Aleck Ostry, MA, MSc, PhD
Assistant Professor, Department of
Health Care and Epidemiology
University of British Columbia
ostry@interchange.ubc.ca

Joyce Slater
184 Chestnut Street
Winnipeg MB
R3G 1R6
jslater@mts.net
204-774-5563
and **Pat Bugera-Krawchuk**
Manitoba Milk Producers
P.O. Box 724
Winnipeg MB
R3C 2K3
204- 488-6455

Laura Kalina, R.D.N., M.Ad.Ed.
Registered Dietitian
Manager, Shop Smart Tours
email: shopsmart@telus.net
Ph/Fax: 250-372-0815

Debbie Field
Executive Director
FoodShare Toronto
238 Queen Street West
Toronto ON
M5V 1Z7
416-392-1628
Fax: 416-392-6650
debbie@foodshare.net
www.foodshare.net

Kerniel Aasland
CEDTAS Coordinator
400 B Logan Avenue,
Winnipeg MB
R3A 0R1
204-927-9921
Fax: 204-586-7820
cedtas@seedwinnipeg.ca

Peter Katona
Executive Director
Foodlink Waterloo Region
Contact: Ellen Desjardins, MHSc, RD
Public Health Nutritionist
Region of Waterloo Public Health
99 Regina St. S., 3rd floor
Waterloo ON
N2J 4V3
519-883-2004 ext 5166
Fax: 519-883-2241
dellen@region.waterloo.on.ca

Patty Williams
Assistant Professor
Department of Applied Human Nutrition
Mount Saint Vincent University
166 Bedford Highway
Halifax NS
B3M 2J6
902-457-6394
Fax: 902-457-6134
patty.williams@msvu.ca
www.ahprc.dal.ca/www.nsnc.ca/www.foodthoughtful.ca

Elizabeth Brims
Executive Director
York Region Food Network
194 Eagle Street
Newmarket ON L3Y 1J6
905-967-0428
yrfn@bellnet.ca
www.yrfn.ca

Notes

Notes